Undies

Undies to Equities

From refugee to financial guru,
the remarkable life of

Henri Aram

With Michael Visontay

ROSENBERG

First published in Australia in 2012
by Rosenberg Publishing Pty Ltd
PO Box 6125, Dural Delivery Centre NSW 2158
Phone: 61 2 9654 1502 Fax: 61 2 9654 1338
Email: rosenbergpub@smartchat.net.au
Web: www.rosenbergpub.com.au

National Library of Australia Cataloguing-in-Publication entry

Author: Aram, Henri

Title: Undies to equities : from refugee to financial guru, the remarkable life of Henri Aram / Henri Aram ; Michael Visontay.

ISBN: 9781921719547 (pbk.)

Notes: Includes index.
Subjects: Aram, Henri.
Investment advisors--Australia--Biography.
Financial planners--Australia--Biography.
Businesspeople--Australia--Biography.
Business enterprises--Australia--History.
Finance, Personal--Australia.
Jewish children--Germany--Biography.
Germans--Australia--Biography.
Aliens--Australia--Biography.
Immigrants--Australia--Biography.

Other Authors/Contributors: Visontay, Michael.

Dewey Number: 332.02400994

Set in 12 on 16 point Arno Pro
Printed in China by Everbest Printing Co Limited

CONTENTS

DEDICATION AND ACKNOWLEDGMENTS

This book is dedicated to my wife Robin for her patience and endurance to continue living with me during the years it took to get this book to completion, and for having to listen to the stories of my life over and over again.

Grateful acknowledgment to Robin's two sons Jason and Marcus, and also to my nephews Anthony and Alexander in Tokyo, for their ongoing encouragement in my writing the family story, my memoirs for them and their growing families.

To Michael Visontay, for his intense prompting to tell him the stories of my life as they came to mind or to recall long-forgotten events that shaped my career. Without Michael's expertise in getting me to open up and even reveal some of my best-kept secrets, this book would never have seen the light of day.

To Aubrey Pomerance, head of Archives at the Leo Baeck Institute, part of the Jewish Museum in Berlin, for his helpfulness and generosity in providing archival photos and other valuable information.

To Bruce Hill, who solved the naming conundrum for the book by spotting the title in one of my writings.

Finally, a loving tribute to my adoptive grandfather, Moritz Sachs, affectionately known as Onkel Mor, who gave what was left of his life savings after the Nazis plundered most of his wealth, to enable my immediate family to flee the Nazi terror. Without his financial contribution, all the family would have become a mere statistic amongst the millions killed by a murderous regime, and no family history or memoirs of my life could have been written.

Henri Aram

PROLOGUE

June is an optimistic month in Germany. The days are long and warm, the sun sets late and the summer has yet to unfold fully. It is a time of renewal. In 1998, my family and friends gathered in a Berlin cemetery from across the world to renew a relationship, and pay tribute to someone whose debt had not been paid back.

My brother Arnold and his wife flew in from Japan, I came with my wife Robin from Sydney, my lifelong friend Fred Nomburg came from Israel, and my niece journeyed from another part of Germany – to consecrate a memorial stone to Moritz Sachs, better known as Onkel Mor. We were joined by the Mayor of Weissensee and a representative of the Schultheiss company Onkel Mor had served so faithfully until he was betrayed by the Nazis.

I was 75, my brother was 77. Onkel Mor saved us and our parents from the Nazis in the lead-up to the war but for too long we had no way of recognising his generosity and self-sacrifice. However, when the Berlin Wall came down in 1989 I saw an opportunity, finally, to show him the respect he deserved.

It took me nearly ten years to find Onkel Mor's final resting place and organise this ceremony. His grave was hard to find and there were many complications along the way. German protocols and regulations came back to haunt me once again. So too did the customs of Jewish tradition.

But now it was happening. As we stood around the memorial in the Weissensee Cemetery, listening to speeches from the Mayor and others, I wished my parents could have been standing alongside. Both my father and my mother, so close to Onkel Mor in different ways, would have loved to know that we did this.

The *Sydney Morning Herald* had a correspondent in Berlin at the time, Geoff Kitney, who I invited to the ceremony, and he interviewed me afterwards. 'For me, this is the completion of a journey … a happy, sad day,' I told him. 'I wanted this to be a ceremony of reconciliation, and I am very pleased that is what it was.'

Thirteen years later, as I approach my ninetieth birthday, I can now look back on the fulfilling and surprising life I have lived thanks to the actions of Onkel Mor 70 years ago. With this book, I have tried to capture the highs and lows in my journey from Berlin to Sydney and my new start in Australia. There have been unexpected pleasures and pain, the refugee's hurdles and the migrant's capacity for hard work and eye for an opportunity. But for me, Australia has indeed been the Lucky Country. Here is my story.

ONE-WAY TICKET

At the break of dawn on 9 November 1938, on a cold, grey autumn morning, my family waited impatiently outside our apartment in Berlin for two taxis to arrive. One was for my father and my older brother Arnold, and me. The other was for my mother and my grandfather, who we called Onkel Mor. Arnold was seventeen and I was fifteen; we looked at each other nervously while the neighbourhood slowly woke up. We looked around at our home, the suburb, which we were about to leave, never knowing when we would return.

A few people were on the streets, their heads bent forward in the cold, moving quickly to their destinations. The taxis arrived and we got in quickly. We had just one suitcase between us. 'To the train station,' my father instructed the taxi drivers briskly.

Half an hour later, we pulled up at the Lehrter Bahnhof, where my mother, brother and I were booked on a train for Hamburg, and then a boat to Grimsby and on to Liverpool in the north of England. The station was familiar; we had used it several times in the past few years when our family had taken trips. But now it was different: everywhere around us Nazi soldiers walked around with hard looks on their faces, arms flying up in Sieg Heil salutes. Their distinctive brown shirts turned the waiting room into something more like a military barracks.

My mother and father looked at each other anxiously, willing the minutes to tick by so the train could take us to safety. I thought I was calm but the gravity of the situation got to me and I suddenly felt an overwhelming urge to use the toilet. In the circumstances, this was awkward enough for a small fifteen-year-old boy. But I had never been to a public toilet before. We had been brought up in an affluent neighbourhood and our apartment was within walking distance from every school I had ever been to.

My father looked calm but preoccupied. He was under enough stress so I played it cool.

'Can I have ten pfennigs for the toilet, Father?' I asked quietly.

He gave me the coins and I walked quickly down to the toilet. Now my nerves took over. Afraid of locking myself in, I tested the door to the room. It clicked and unclicked. Good. I put my ten pfennigs in; the door opened, then closed and locked itself. I was pleased with how I had handled this strange environment, unaware I needed to put in another coin to open it again.

I decided to try the door again, just to be sure. This time it didn't open. I shook the door and the handle furiously but nothing happened. Why was it okay the first two times but not now? A shiver of fear swept down my spine. I was locked in, and the train was going to leave shortly. Trickles of sweat broke out on my forehead and when a beggar came in to ask for money I pleaded with him, agitated: 'Please, could you help me?' He turned away without response. It dawned on me that I was on my mother's passport and if I didn't get out soon she would leave without me, and I would be stuck in Germany. I had no idea how to get out; my head felt like it was about to explode.

I don't know how long I had been in the toilet when suddenly I heard the sweetest sound: 'Heinz! Heinz! Are you there?' my father shouted. (Heinz was my original German name.) I relaxed and slumped to the seat. He fiddled with the door and in a few minutes I was out in the strangely comforting noise of the train station. My father never got excited, but on this occasion he was visibly upset. 'You open and close the door, then it locks itself,' he explained as we walked back to the others. My father hadn't thought to tell me beforehand and I didn't know to ask. After that we walked back in silence. I never went for a piddle but I made the train. To this day I still wake up at night, wondering what would have happened if my father hadn't come over to look for me. In those days, it was common for children to be kidnapped and who knows where I might have ended up?

Around us the station was a hive of activity: families dragging suitcases along the platforms, kids screaming while their parents cajoled them into the carriages, parents hugging children who were leaving. All the while, soldiers eyed the travellers suspiciously, as though we were committing a crime simply by being there, by wanting to get away from the intolerable world of Nazism outside.

Our goodbye was typically understated. My father was not given to prominent displays of emotion, and neither was Onkel Mor. Perhaps they knew something, too, that they didn't want us to see. We already knew why they couldn't come with us: they were too old. My father was 62, and Onkel Mor was 65, a few years over the limit for the landing permits in Australia that the three of us had received after months of anxious negotiation. But was there some other piece of information the three grown-ups were hiding from us? My parents embraced, and Onkel Mor hugged my mother. Turning to my brother and me, they gave us firm handshakes and a hand on the shoulder. We walked up the steps out of the station and we turned around to face the future. But first, we faced the people in our compartment, a couple named Rosen with a little girl called Jutta (who many years later would become the mother of Philip Stricker, now a prominent Sydney urologist). The child had been farewelled by their grandparents; her grandfather collapsed on the station, possibly with a stroke, when the train pulled out. It was a terrible thing to see and felt like a bad omen for our trip. (We heard later that the grandparents were later deported.)

From Hamburg, we sailed for several hours to Grimsby in the north-east of England. The next day we were taken to Liverpool. That is where we first read the news about what had happened while we were in transit overnight. November 9, 1938 was Kristallnacht, the 'Night of the Broken Glass', when German stormtroopers ransacked Jewish shops and businesses, burned synagogues and shattered the windows of Jewish shops. Arnold and I were bewildered. In all of the uncertainty and declarations by the Nazis over the past five years, we could not imagine something like this. My mother was beside herself. 'What has happened to your father and Onkel Mor?' she wailed. It was the same day and details were sketchy. Had they even got home alright, she wondered.

My mother's fears were well-founded. Back in Berlin, my father and Onkel Mor came home from the train station to a bare apartment which they could not leave due to the mayhem on the streets outside. The furniture from our roomy apartment had been removed and packed for shipment to Australia. But when it arrived at the wharf a couple of weeks later, they were forced to pay an absurd tax of 20 per cent of the value of the furniture: a Reichsfluchtsteuer, which was a tax 'to flee the country'. The transport company told them it would not ship the goods to Australia until the penalty was paid. It was an enormous sum, which cleared out their entire bank accounts. This was after they had mustered 30,000 deutschmarks for the £200 they had to pay for our Australian landing permits.

To make matters worse, Onkel Mor's pension was stopped the day after Kristallnacht, a calamity for us. Mor occupied a unique role in our family. He was not a blood relation but a close business friend of my father who introduced him to my mother, then later legally adopted her when her own father died. His money, generosity, and more recently his so-called lifetime pension from the large brewing company he worked for, had kept our family afloat through all the problems of the past few years. On 10 November he received a blunt, formal letter from his old company, Schultheiss Patzenhofer: 'From this day on your pension has been cancelled, with immediate effect.' No explanation, no other sentiments. My father was stoic, it took a lot to bring him down. Onkel Mor was devastated. His security for the future, the one lifeline that gave him reason to believe he could survive life in Nazi Germany, had been destroyed without warning.

We knew none of this at the time. With Germany disintegrating behind us, and no way to contact my father, all my mother could do was focus on the journey ahead. We stayed in the small port of Grimsby overnight, then travelled to Liverpool for a day or so, just in time to board our ticket to safety: the *Duchess of Bedford*, a sturdy Canadian-built vessel which I later learnt was apparently renowned for its seaworthiness. At the time all I cared about was that it floated. We were placed in what they called steerage class; below the waterline. It was effectively third class, we shared a cabin, and there was a sort of dining room that had benches; no chairs. It was rough, as you would expect from third class. But we were in no position, or mind, to complain.

The *Duchess of Bedford* set sail for Canada and after several days of rough seas, uncomfortable quarters but clean food and water, we were met in Montreal by hundreds of Russian immigrants who had moved there a few years earlier. Because we were the first ship to arrive after the

Kristallnacht, we had a special aura about us: it seemed to everyone that we would be the last to get out. The locals showered us with money and lollies.

There was still no news about father and Onkel Mor as we began the next stage of our journey: across Canada by train, straight through to the Rockies. We had plenty of well-wishers but just £2 between us. A few days later we were on the west coast of Canada, and put on a boat to Australia via New Zealand. It was called the *Aorangi,* a dilapidated old steamer slightly worse than the *Duchess of Bedford,* which took about three weeks to bring us to the other side of the world. It was a long three weeks for everyone on board, the sea took some getting used to but the journey went without incident. It was reassuring to set foot on dry land in Auckland, where we were met by another group of well-wishers, this time a group of largely German dentists who had been rescued from concentration camps by members of a New Zealand delegation of politicians. They solved an existing shortage of dentists in their country by offering asylum to hundreds of German practitioners, in the process saving them from the gas chambers.

We were also more formally met by a representative of the Jewish Relief Fund from Sydney, a Doctor Matzdorf, whose task was to help the refugees resettle. He boarded the boat on the last leg to Sydney, and during the journey he interviewed us to help organise accommodation, jobs, possessions and anything else.

We arrived in Sydney on 15 December, nearly six weeks after leaving Berlin. It was so hot the ground shimmered with heat. The light was fierce, harsher than the soft summer light of Europe. It felt like a furnace and we boys wondered what sort of country we had entered. Silently, my mother wondered what had happened to father and Onkel Mor, of whom we still had no news.

They had struggled to pick up the pieces of their life in Berlin. My father lost his job, and with Onkel Mor's pension stopped they had no money and no reasonable prospect for getting any. Yet in the midst of this chaos, my father retained a sense of defiant bravado. On Kristallnacht, after we left Berlin and the Nazis went on their rampage through the streets of Germany, he bought a French newspaper and walked along the streets to survey the damage. Our neighbourhood was mainly empty, there was hardly anyone on the street. My father stood out, he was a target. The police came over, noticed the French paper and asked him what he was doing. 'I'm French. What's happened?' he replied abruptly. 'Get on your way,' they told him.

My father loved to challenge authority, and for this act of chutzpah he was rewarded with an unexpected stroke of luck – a rescue from relatives in Sweden. Just as his passport was about to expire and he thought he would be stuck in Germany, he received an invitation to visit Sweden. 'We'll guarantee you,' they wrote.

My father's uncle had a daughter who he married off, several years earlier, to a very wealthy family in Stockholm. She had two sons, his cousins, who were extremely generous, decent people. One of them came to Germany from Sweden during the war – on a visa granted by the Swedish King Gustaf – to pick up an elderly aunt of my father's, 90-year-old Aunt Felice. Whenever they went on holiday, they visited King Gustaf who had a villa in the South of France.

Their generosity, wealth and contacts saved my father at this crucial time. With only a few days left on his passport, he left for Sweden and arrived there with about ten marks in his pocket. His sense of fortune only increased when the German Consulate in Sweden wouldn't renew his passport, because they had information that he had officially changed his name, which was true (from Abraham to Aram, in 1931). He stayed, relieved that he made it out just in time, and from Stockholm eventually made his way to Australia.

Onkel Mor was not so lucky. He stayed in Germany after my father left, too old and too sick to flee. Onkel Mor had a heart condition, he was totally impoverished and knew that if he was caught trying to leave he could expect deportation to a fate he didn't want to think about. Faced with an impossible scenario, he took a room in a modest area while our housekeeper, Hedwig, and his former secretary from Schultheiss, Fraulein Gumpert, looked after him. Onkel Mor was totally dependent on them. The two women did their best to make his life bearable. Hedwig risked her life for him. By that stage Onkel Mor was forced to wear a yellow Magen David badge on his clothes – the Jewish Star of David that Nazis made all Jews wear to humiliate them. Hedwig, a staunch Catholic, made her own Magen David to accompany him when needed, so the authorities would not know that a non-Jew was associating with a Jew. This was now a crime under Nazi laws; if they found out she was not Jewish they would have taken her away.

Despite their brave support, Onkel Mor knew his future was impossible. In March 1940, after eighteen months of living in this captive existence, he took an overdose of the tablets he was taking for his heart condition. It wasn't officially recognised as suicide but that is certainly what it was, one of many 'enforced suicides' that German Jews felt was the only way out under Nazism. After the war we saw many headstones and memorials to other Jews who saw this as the only option available to them. The cremation and burial were arranged by Fraulein Gumpert, and his ashes were laid to rest two months later – with no reason ever given for the two-month delay.

In 1940, when we were in Australia, we received a cable through the Red Cross from my step-grandmother: 'We're well, are you well? Your brother Heinrich and Onkel Mor are dead.' That was the only thing we ever heard about his death. The cable from my step-grandmother arrived the week before she was deported to Auschwitz, along with her daughter Hannah, where they and Hannah's children were killed in the gas chambers.

THE BOYS FROM BRESLAU

My mother and father both came from the area around Breslau, which was a town on German–Polish border. Every time there was a war it changed nationalities depending on who won. My father always told us that 'all good Berliners come from Breslau'. He was in his forties, and a bachelor, when he met my mother, in her twenties, courtesy of Onkel Mor. Born in Breslau in 1873, just three years before my father, Onkel Mor was unable to have children following a major bowel operation as a young man and had never married. He became a very successful businessman; Mor owned retail stores in Breslau, an apartment block, and later became a director of the large German brewery Schultheiss Patzenhofer AG, which is how he met my father.

Both men were in the commodities business – my father was a partner in a coffee roasting business called Rudolph Fabisch and Co. He was considered such an expert that he was called on to judge disputes about coffee and beans. Through his involvement in the beer industry, Mor had to purchase grain for the brewing process. Over the years their businesses brought them together in meetings and markets, and they struck up a close friendship.

Mor also knew of my mother, and her family, through intertwining social circles. One day he introduced my parents to each other. There was a considerable age difference between them. My father was 44, and my mother 24 when they married in Beuthen, Upper Silesia, in 1920. Brought up in a smaller area outside Breslau, she was born Rosa Riesenfeld, the youngest of six children – four girls and two boys. The eldest was Heinrich, then came Mietze, followed by Elsa, Charlotte, Alfred and then Rosa. Her mother died while giving birth to her. The consequences of this tragedy were many: for a start my mother's birthday, New Year's eve, was always an occasion of sadness because it was the same day her mother died, and in her own mind she was the cause of her death. Secondly, her father, a builder, married again and had another two children, Friedl and Hannah. Rosa had a good relationship with her stepmother, Bertha, but the other sisters did not.

One day Rosa's father won a large sum of money in a State lottery – 5000 deutschmarks. He used the money to start building the first apartment block in the town. Before the building was finished there was a very heavy snowfall. The snow collected on the roof, and when it thawed a big block of ice fell and killed a woman passerby. He was not insured, so he lost all the money he won in the lottery in compensation to the woman's family. The incident left him weak and dispirited. Soon after, he had a heart attack and died. After his friend's death, and with no family of his own, Onkel Mor took an interest in my mother and her five siblings. He became her de facto father, a role he formalised in 1935 when he adopted my mother and made her two sons, Arnold and me, the beneficiaries of his estate.

Because my father was considerably older, his parents were both dead by the time I was born. He did have a younger sister, who I never met.

All I knew was that she was crippled. My father said that when his sister was a baby, her nurse dropped her. My father looked after her, and she died in her forties. From that side, we had no surviving family.

My mother's family more than made up for his; they were a colourful clan. Her sister Charlotte was an attractive, headstrong girl who didn't get on with her stepmother, and at the age of seventeen she jumped on the train to Vienna where she found a job as nursemaid to the then American Ambassador to Austria. He took her wherever he travelled. On one of these trips she met a rich diamond merchant and formed a relationship with him, which some years later took them to Palestine, a hub of the global diamond trade. They stayed at the glamorous King David Hotel in Jerusalem, where they fought and broke up. Charlotte was distraught; her life was in tatters – but not for long. An Australian grazier, a widower of Russian Jewish background who had fled the Russian Revolution and made a fortune on the other side of the world, spied her in the lobby and took pity on her. 'Why don't you come to Australia?' he said. 'Here's the money for a ticket. Relax and enjoy the journey.' The grazier said he would continue his business trip in Europe and they would meet when he got home.

Others might see this as a set-up. To Charlotte, it was fate knocking at the door. She had ridden her luck so far, and had nothing to lose. She accepted his offer of a first-class ticket by ocean liner to Sydney. The grazier turned up as planned, showed her his mansion in the exclusive harbourside locality of Clifton Gardens near Mosman, and they were married around the turn of the century, even though he was much older than Charlotte (a family trait that emerged in many of our marriages).

In 1923, just after I was born, the couple visited Berlin with a shipload of wool, the proceeds of which he left to my mother and her elder sister, Mietze. (That money, of course, disappeared in the Depression.) 'Why don't you come to Australia, and I'll set you up in a coffee business,' he said to my father. But my father wasn't moving:

'I have two children, I have a great business here.' This was the first of many moments of fate in my life. My father could have – should have – gone to Australia when he first had the opportunity. But then I would have missed out on the life I have been privileged to live.

Charlotte and her husband booked into the fashionable Hotel Adlon in the heart of Berlin. A party was arranged for her family and my father told us how she turned heads when she entered the room in an evening gown adorned with Australian ostrich feathers. In the ground-floor foyer the first Mercedes convertible was on display. Just what Charlotte needed, so her husband, Uncle Michael, commissioned my father to buy the car and ship it to Australia. It was to prove the first 'bottom of the harbour' job. Shortly after its delivery to their waterfront home, Charlotte forgot to put on the hand brake and the car rolled down their steep driveway into the harbour. The car was salvaged and restored and is now held in the collection of an established vintage car dealer.

Although my mother was the youngest of the six children, she was a dominant force among them. Perhaps the loss of her own mother during her birth left a scar. Certainly, she could never celebrate her birthday because her mother died on the same day. This was compounded by the death of her oldest sister Elsa, who had been a volunteer nursing sister during World War I. While still in her early twenties, Elsa attended to the wounded at the front line and hospitals in East Prussia and Russia. She paid the supreme sacrifice for her country and died from an infection shortly before the end of the war in 1918.

While the other siblings would socialise, my mother would study dressmaking, bra-making, cosmetics. Her diligence and these skills ultimately saved our lives. She became the breadwinner and assumed responsibility for the others, particularly so with her older sister Mietze, who was the plainest of the girls, which prompted my mother to put an advertisement in the papers to find her a husband. My father's coffee business was in a street called Rosenthaler Strasse so my mother put that as the address to reply to. They received a letter from an Orthodox Jewish man whose name happened to be Rosenthal, who had just lost his wife, and was raising their son by himself. He saw the names as an omen, they hit it off and became a wonderful couple. The boy, Franz, took to his new mother like a house on fire. Alas, this story had a sad ending. Although Franz went to become a rabbi in Chicago, Mietze and her husband, Heinrich Rosenthal, perished in Auschwitz. They were the first to be killed in the gas chambers in the presence of Himmler, according to my cousin Franz. The German government, after the war, awarded Franz a medal as compensation (which I wouldn't have accepted).

My mother also urged her step-sister Friedl, who was living with her mother in the small town of Mislowitz near Breslau, to come to Berlin, and advertised to get a husband for her. A widower, also with one child, a daughter, answered the ad and took her on as a housekeeper. Eventually he married her, and she became Mrs Ranzehoff. However, her husband, Professor Ranzehoff, was a very hot-tempered man. When the Nazis came to power he stood on his balcony during a large street parade and shouted: 'Hitler is a murderer.' My father packed them off that same night on a train out of the country. They eventually went to South Africa. Professor Ranzehoff, who changed his name to Ransome, spoke half a dozen languages, including Afrikaans, and worked as an interpreter. Shortly before the outbreak of war he became naturalised in South Africa and went back to Britain where he joined the army and rose to the rank of captain. After the war he worked as an interpreter at the Nuremberg war trials.

Heinrich, the eldest brother, held great sway with my mother. His wife Gustl had become addicted to morphine after an operation, and Heinrich decided to put her into an asylum. My mother spoke up and Gustl came to live in the maid's room. She went to the chemist and arranged with him to substitute milk for morphine in her capsules. For about a year, they fed her these capsules, and the strategy worked: Gustl was cured of the addiction. Before the war broke out Heinrich and Gustl intended to migrate to Brazil. Their two sons, both academics, were already working abroad – one in Switzerland, the other in Brazil. The one in South America sent them a permit which would allow them to land there; it was very hard to obtain landing permits at that time. But when they boarded the ship in Hamburg they found that the visa was falsified; the shock of this news gave Heinrich a heart attack and he died. Gustl made her way to South America alone.

My mother's youngest brother, Alfred, was theatrical in every way. He trained as a Shakespearean actor (having changed his name to Gorton) and married a vivacious Russian actress, Sonia. The marriage of two actors was turbulent and it was no surprise when they divorced. In the 1920s Alfred managed the thriving Picture Theatres (Kinos) in Berlin, which provided my brother and me with free matinees. As the Nazis took power, he went on a tour to Australia and may have performed at the Theatre Royal in Sydney. His wife also performed, on a different stage, and it was later rumoured that she had an affair with Charlotte's (Russian-born) husband and contributed to their divorce. Alfred later migrated to the United States, retired on a pension and then went to live in Perth, with visits to his families in Sydney during the 1970s.

My father's grandparents

My mother's father

My mother's mother

My father in his uniform as a wireless officer during World War I

My mother at the time of her marriage

My mother as a young girl

My father at his favourite pastime, rowing on the Wansee

My mother (right) with her step-sister Hannah, later murdered with her family in Auschwitz

My parents shortly after they were married

My mother as a young girl with her oldest sister Mietze

My mother's oldest sister, Mieze, before departation

My mother's second oldest sister, Elsa, who died as a volunteer nurse in 1918

My first day at school, with the traditional 'Sugarhorn of plenty'

My mother with her two sons, Arnold (left) and me, at the Lietzensee

Ice skating with my brother on the Lietzensee, 1933

In character with Arnold for a pantomime at the wedding of my Aunt Friedl

The Lietzensee and park on a sunny summer's day

My school class in 1929 with our teacher, later killed in Auschwitz

At Zopot, a seaside resort near Danzig, with my mother and brother, in 1933. The swimming outfits were made by my mother.

NOT QUITE AN APRIL FOOL

I was born into a family of middle-class German Jews in Berlin on 2 April 1923, the second son of Julius and Rosa Abraham. My brother Arnold was two years older than me. During my infant years, Germany was still in turmoil in the aftermath of World War I, and the reparations imposed by the Treaty of Versailles. With the economy reeling due to hyperinflation in the early 1920s, Hitler attempted his beer hall putsch in 1923, shortly after I was born. When I was old enough to start school, Germany was engulfed by the Depression.

However, by this time my parents were reasonably comfortable. My father owned a Mercedes, a chauffeur drove him around in his business and my mother did not need to work. This was a far cry from their early married years, when they got around on a three-wheeled bicycle wearing leather jackets and helmets. They made a dashing pair. My mother used to tell us that whenever my father went round a corner the bike used to tip up, which scared her.

We lived in the west of Berlin in a suburb named Charlottenburg, in a spacious apartment built around a courtyard, opposite a very large park and lake called Lietzensee. The apartment was large enough to accommodate live-in help; it included a maid's room and a nursery. The building was quite fashionable in its day, as was the suburb; our neighbours included an engineer with Mercedes. His name was Maybach and many years later Mercedes named one of its luxury models after him.

In summertime we went swimming, in the winter time we had ice skating. School was around the corner and we walked there every day, a habit I tried to maintain – walking daily – for much of my life. We had a housekeeper, and a nurse for the children. The nurse used to take us, first in the pram and then walking, in the park, and then walk us around to school.

For holidays we often used to go to the farm of our nurse's parents. She was part of the family, so much so that when we got older my mother sent her to England to learn English. On her return, she started to teach us English while we were still in Germany. Our housekeeper, Hedwig, came to us as a young girl of nineteen and stayed with us until Hitler came to power. Under the Nuremberg laws of 1935 she was prevented from working with a Jewish family but she defied the rules and she stayed with us for more than fifteen years, coming to the house after dark when she could not longer live with us.

Arnold and I were brought up in a typical German way: children were seen and not heard. Until we were ten, we never sat at the dining room table with our parents. We used to eat before them, only speak when we were asked to, and were never allowed to read the paper before our parents did. We were brought up strictly, and that proved a handicap. In my early years, and later as a young man, I did not have the confidence to speak in public; I had been denied that life skill as part of my upbringing and I regretted its absence many times over. As children, when we were asked to reply to questions, we always had to be very polite to visitors, but we weren't allowed to partake in discussions at the dinner table until asked. We had our dinner with a maid, with a nurse in our room – that was the German way. But it was a happy, harmonious life; we never wanted for anything.

My mother's first priority was for us to get a good education. It was something both parents valued. We were never encouraged in sports because my parents did not consider sport as essential as education. They lived comfortably but modestly, and did not throw big parties or celebrations. My parents focused completely on the children, our education, our home. When it came to schools, this was translated into careful research about which was the right school for the two sons, each carefully picked according to the strengths they saw in us from an early age.

My brother went to the Kaiser Wilhelm Gymnasium, a technical high school. One of his schoolmates was the son of Joseph Goebbels, later Hitler's Minister for Propaganda, until the time Jews were thrown out. I went to the American school in Berlin, which was run under the patronage of the American Embassy (and had the extra benefit of being on American territory, in case anything untoward happened politically). We studied French and English; we even had home teaching after school.

Yet even here, in this seemingly safe environment, the outside world intruded into our lives. One of my tutors was a Frau von Mueller, a striking-looking woman in her fifties who was born in England and married to a World War I German submarine captain. Frau von Mueller seemed to be well connected with every nationality and political group. She had excellent teaching credentials, having been recommended by the American Embassy to teach English, but she was also known to be invited to parties thrown by Hitler and Goering. She was a good teacher but as a young boy I always felt she had a sinister personality, probably exaggerated by the fact that she always wore a large cape. She seemed enveloped by it, and this made her seem shadowy, as though she was hiding something. We saw a lot of her through my lessons, and my mother invited her over for coffee one afternoon.

She didn't turn up, of course. Her links with the German military meant she could not go to a Jewish home. There were rumours that she was a spy, possibly a double agent, pretending to be pro-Nazi but secretly working for the Allies. Frau von Mueller had a beautiful daughter, of whom she was fiercely protective. One of my English lessons with her was cancelled suddenly after her daughter was brutally bashed and taken to hospital. She once declared that 'If war ever breaks out, we will escape to Norway.'

The speculation about her sympathies was also prompted by the strange life of her husband, who spent several years in the lead-up to the war living in Scotland as a watchmaker. The rumour in Berlin was that he had been sent there as an undercover agent, a sleeper, whose maritime knowledge we later heard was utilised in the Nazi attack on the British naval base at Scapa Flow in the Orkney Islands in Scotland. In October 1939, the German U-boat U-47 infiltrated Scapa Flow and sank the British battleship HMS *Royal Oak,* which was anchored there. The U-boat fired a volley of torpedos, one of which blew a huge hole in the *Royal Oak* which flooded and quickly capsized. Of its 1400-man crew, 833 were lost. I never found out what happened to either Captain or Frau Von Mueller.

Another teacher from my school also became secretly involved in the war. He was English, his name was Jones and he wasn't married. Every so often Mr Jones would disappear from the school, without explanation, then return as though nothing had happened. Years later, in Australia, my father showed me newspaper reports that Mr Jones had been helping young Jewish women escape from the Nazis by arranging fake marriages and taking them to England. Eventually, he was caught and put into jail by the Nazis.

When Hitler came to power, the Depression had already ruined my father's import/export coffee business. Not that it alarmed him; he never worried about anything. I was only ten at the time and his calmness left a firm imprint on me. His attitude to life was philosophical: 'what happens, happens,' he would say. My father always found a way out. Somehow.

Perhaps his confidence lay in the fact that he was an excellent, instinctive salesman. After the business folded, he sold legal publications for a while and tried a few other jobs, but it wasn't until my father met Emil Bauer from the Hannovera Registrierkassen cash register company that he found something he really believed in. He travelled the whole of Germany to sell cash registers. Mr Bauer was a model boss to my father; I still have references from him, he contacted us after the war, having survived with his son. In fact, the firm is still in existence.

In a climate of fear and paranoia, old friends stopped talking, childhood playmates became enemies and Jewish-sounding names became a liability, so much so that in 1931 my parents officially changed their surname from Abraham to Aram. The authorities decreed that name changes would only be approved if the original letters in the former name were retained in the alteration. (For this I owe a small measure of gratitude: later in life this four-letter name would become my logo for many business activities.)

While my father was trying to make ends meet after he lost his business, my mother announced that she had contacts in Paris, most likely through her sister Charlotte. The senile President Hindenburg made Hitler Chancellor in 1933, just before my tenth birthday, and soon afterwards my mother went off to Paris, alone, on a fact-finding trip. She met a French Jewish gentleman there. 'I have a business in making clothing,' he told her. 'I'll set you up as a subsidiary and you will make children's school uniforms.'

The German Jews never believed Hitler would survive for long. They thought the regime would collapse. Instead, it grew more powerful and life became more oppressive. They used to joke: 'the difference between Hitler and the Messiah is that the Messiah won't come and Hitler won't go!' With the Nazi threat rising, my mother was keen to seek out any opportunity that might save her family. She accepted the offer and established a business in Paris, then sent word back for us to join her. As my father's work situation was relatively fragile, we followed in 1934, with our housekeeper Hedwig, settling in a modern apartment block in the Rue Villiers de Lille Adam in the 20th arrondissement. It was a comfortable flat of about three bedrooms, not far from the Place de la Republique, where my mother had her business. Soon we two boys acquired enough French to follow our classes. My father ran the dress factory, and with the help of an American-born local called Monsieur Facteur (a designer and cutter by trade), life ran relatively smoothly.

Why did my mother decide to uproot herself and the family and go to Paris? For a start, she was blessed with great energy and drive, as demonstrated by the way she took responsibility for her older sisters. However, the Nazi policies had also struck uncomfortably close to home, which changed her long-term outlook profoundly.

One of Hitler's first measures as Chancellor in 1933 was to take big companies that had substantial numbers of Jewish board members and subtly undermine them – for example, by accusing the directors of defrauding the company. The Nazis appointed a new secretary of state whose job was to supervise and monitor companies' performances. One of the companies that came under the spotlight was Schultheiss Patzenhofer, where Onkel Mor worked as a director. It was at that time the largest brewery in Germany and had recently taken over a milling company that supplied it with a lot of the malt and products as part of the supply chain for beer production.

Schultheiss had several Jewish directors on the board and the Nazis trumped up a fraud scandal against the company, which the papers portrayed as a Jewish fraud. My grandfather, who had been with the company for 36 years, was very prominent in Schultheiss. What became known as the 'Schultheiss scandal' (also known as the Katzenellenbogen Skandal, after the company chairman's name) caused a huge upheaval in our family because Onkel Mor's reputation was smeared even though nothing was ever proven. The secretary of state, who orchestrated this whole enquiry and declared the company had been defrauded, hid the fact that the director of finance of the company was none other than Hjalmar Schacht, who was to become Hitler's Minister for Economics. The case never went to court. The company's chairman, Mr Katzenellenbogen, fled to Greece, and when the Germans invaded Greece they caught him and brought him back to Germany. He was never tried but was murdered by the Nazis.

This affair caused my mother to reassess the whole situation. She could see clearly that there would be no future for Jews in Germany. It brought the political uncertainty close to home because it was so personal. The scandal hit us hard. My brother and I were only boys at the time but we knew there was something happening because we could see that Onkel Mor was very troubled. It was never discussed in front of us but we could read the papers and we listened to the radio.

GREY PAREE

Shortly after our arrival in Paris both my mother and I encountered health issues. My mother complained of a bowel problem that suggested an urgent operation. Thankfully, she recovered without needing surgery. Soon after, I had an emergency appendix operation which left me with a serious kidney problem which a German doctor in Paris misdiagnosed. With the help of a French doctor who recommended a daily diet of half a small bottle of French sauterne, I improved without permanent addiction or other side effects.

In Paris we went to the École Alsacienne, where we could speak German as well as French. Although there was severe political unrest around us – on the way to school we saw buses burned and overturned – Arnold and I enjoyed living in France because my mother's sister, Charlotte, had moved to Nice on the Côte d'Azur after her marriage had broken up in the late 1920s. She lived in the glamorous Negresco Hotel, home to the rich and famous, she was very comfortably off and she invited us to come down to visit her. We were so impressed by the money and manners of life down on the Riviera. My aunt had a little Pekingese dog, Winky, who she brought to the restaurant when she was being served a meal. Winky was served her meal separately. We loved the ocean in Nice. That was new. And so, our life in France was comparatively comfortable. Nevertheless, despite the income my mother brought in, the household was essentially subsidised by Onkel Mor's pension. His forced retirement from the Schultheiss board, at the age of just 59, kept us going for years. He always lived with us, staying in a separate study and bedroom. I remember him fondly. Unfortunately, he didn't like to be photographed so I have no photos of him.

One morning our little world was shattered when Monsieur Facteur, the American-born designer and now friend, walked up the three flights of stairs to the factory office, sat down on the lounge and died of a heart attack. Death is always sad, but in France it meant disaster for us. The ambulance would not attend until police released the body, no one could leave the premises until police had finished their inquiries. Everyone was interviewed and Hedwig, who did not have a work permit, was arrested and taken to jail. My parents eventually provided the sureties and Hedwig was released, which was a joy and relief to the whole family.

The loss of Monsieur Facteur destabilised the business and the stress took its toll on my mother's health. At the same time, the Nazi Minister Hermann Goering published an appeal in the French papers for German Jews to return home, with promises of restitution for seizure of property and loss of jobs. Onkel Mor consulted his friend and former colleague, Dr Schacht, now Hitler's Finance Minister, who confirmed the offer was genuine. 'Nothing gets eaten as hot as it's cooked,' he said to Onkel Mor, and encouraged our family to return to Berlin. My parents were cautious and discussed the idea that the two boys would stay on in Paris at boarding school, which I strongly opposed. In hindsight, returning to Berlin saved my life as we would have been caught in the Nazi invasion of Paris in 1940 and faced deportation to the camps.

By1936 we returned to Berlin and moved into a comfortable five-bedroom apartment in the fashionable Grunewald district. We lived in relative security, amazingly, thanks to the fact that there was a general from Hitler's SA living on our floor who didn't object to Jews. My father resumed his position with the Hannovera cash register company, my mother returned to her cosmetics and beauty training, I was enrolled in the American School and when this became too expensive we switched to the nearby private Jewish school (Lesler Schule). We now spoke decent French and passable English. We also had some other Jewish boys staying with us. Because we lived close to our new school, together with the fact that Jewish students in country areas could no longer attend normal school, my mother decided to take in a couple of Jewish country students who had been forced to attend the Jewish school in Berlin.

We had taken money out of Germany but Onkel Mor insisted we bring it back with us. His ethics were rewarded because we were considered to be devisensicher – 'currency secure'. We weren't considered a flight risk and so the Germans didn't think we were cheating them. If we had left the money over in France, it would have been far more difficult to get it out at the end. The fact that we were prepared to bring it back was considered a vote of confidence in the country.

My father never feared anything, my mother feared everything, and that made life very difficult. I remember my father had a habit of waving to people in a similar way to the Heil Hitler salute. This habit got him into trouble because someone saw him wave, and they sent a letter to him saying that as a Jew he should not use this greeting. My mother was worried that he would be denounced. 'Don't worry,' he would reassure her, which he had to do often.

However, our smooth return to Germany was not to last long. When I celebrated my Bar Mitzvah in 1937 we were not allowed to congregate outside afterwards. We had to go straight home and visitors came to see us. Among them was a Rabbi Sanger, who officiated at the service and then migrated to Australia shortly afterwards and worked at the Temple Beth Israel in St Kilda. I wrote to him early in 1938, asking if he could help us. His curt, brief reply – to my mother instead of me – cut me to the quick.

> I note with great interest that you intend coming to Australia. I would like to draw your attention to the fact that the business man has practically no chance of employment in Australia, whereas people who know a trade … have quite a good chance of earning anything between £3 and £5 a week.
>
> I hope that it will be possible for you to immigrate into Australia. In order to facilitate the proceedings, will you please address yourself to the Jewish Welfare Society.
>
> Yours sincerely,
>
> PS: My regards to your two boys.

Rabbi Sanger had been a mentor and role model to me. I was devastated.

The final implementation of the Nuremberg laws in 1937–38 excluded Jews from all commercial or civic activities. Onkel Mor was forced to dispose of his property holdings on the promise of a settlement when things changed, Emil Bauer was forced to sack my father, and our loyal maid Hedwig had to leave or face prosecution. All cultural centres were closed to Jews, some park benches had yellow 'Jews only' signs painted on them, and even public transport was becoming hazardous for Jews. There was no future for us in our homeland.

Our childhood nurse Ilse, who had always been very good to us, tried to report Hedwig to the authorities. The day the law restricting association between Gentiles and Jews came into effect, Ilse rang and I answered the phone. 'Hello!' I chirped, pleased to hear her voice, but she wouldn't talk to me: she wanted to talk to my mother. I could tell something was wrong because Ilse always used to talk to me. However, she had married a Nazi and bore three children with him. This day she wanted to talk to Hedwig, with whom she had been friendly for years. 'But you know she's not allowed to be here,' I heard my mother saying to Ilse. Then I heard the click as Ilse put the receiver down. I have never forgiven her for that.

After the war Ilse contacted us, asking for help. Her husband was killed in Russia, two of her three children were killed or injured in bomb attacks in Berlin and the surviving one was a cripple. She was living in poverty. I said to my mother: 'Not one cent.' We gave her nothing.

Meanwhile, my family was not about to let Hedwig just slip away. Onkel Mor came to the rescue, again. He often stayed at a boutique Berlin hotel, the Hotel Steinplatz, named after the city precinct, and came to know the staff well. They were looking for a cashier. 'I have a very reliable person,' he told them. Hedwig got the job and advanced to head cashier.

That took care of her job. On the home front, my mother had a wealthy friend, Mrs Chernik, who rented a large apartment near this hotel. 'Why doesn't Hedwig come and stay with me?' she suggested. 'I have this big home, her job is close enough to walk to work.' So Hedwig went and lived with Mrs Chernik. Mrs Chernik vacated the unit and Hedwig applied for the lease. Mrs Chernik kept her in the apartment until 1944 when someone told the police that a Jewish woman was living there. The police searched the unit, arrested Hedwig and sent her to prison. Fortunately, she had formed a relationship with a German count who she met at the hotel, who came to her aid. 'This woman is innocent, I guarantee her,' he told the police. The police released Hedwig from jail on the understanding that she vacate the flat for a war veteran. For her bravery and generosity, poor Mrs Chernik was sent to Auschwitz, where she was murdered. Hedwig was luckier. A couple of months after she left the flat, the whole building was destroyed by a bomb. After the war, Hedwig contacted us and we sent her food parcels. With the furniture she had saved, she later opened her own boutique guest house, Pension Knack (her married name), on the Uhland Strasse.

THE POINT OF NO RETURN

Until 1938 my family clung on to the slim hope that they may still be able to stay in Germany. We children were more or less insulated from what was happening but were old enough at fifteen and seventeen to understand it. Although we read the newspapers and could see how Germany was changing, we were never physically threatened. Years later, when interviewed by schoolchildren at the Jewish Museum about how we had managed to evade any attacks, I could only put it down to luck, and perhaps the location of our flat.

Our villa in Grunewald, after we returned from Paris, was divided into four units: on the ground floor was the Dutch-born director of Philips (also Jewish), and the German countess who owned the whole building. On the first floor, alongside us, lived a high-ranking officer of Hitler's elite guard, an Obersturmführer (whose name I cannot remember) who chose not to object to his Jewish neighbours but also had his staff car and driver guard the property day and night (amazingly, our unit and schools survived the Berlin bombings). This afforded us a level of protection denied to most other Jews. He obviously chose not to take any action against us; this may also have explained why he did not have his name plate on his unit. He did not want anyone to put two and two together.

There was only one specific incident I can remember where I felt physically threatened; it was the day before we left Germany. I came home from the city that day by tram. At one of the stops before I got home, Onkel Mor got on and we were both sitting close to the driver. Ahead of us, a man behind the driver started threatening violence against Jews, in the aftermath of the murder of a German embassy official in Paris.

A seventeen-year-old Polish Jew, Herschel Grynszpan, had gone into the German Embassy in Paris the day before and asked to see an official, any official. He was taken to the office of a man called Ernst von Rath and shot him three times in the stomach, seriously wounding him. The shooting was in retaliation for the news Grynszpan had just heard from his sister. The family, which had emigrated to Germany in 1911 and settled in Hannover, had been rounded up and deported along with other Jewish families late in October. The day after this shooting, 8 November, Hitler ordered all Jewish magazines and newspapers in Germany to stop publishing immediately. With this climate of fear around me, the man's comments in the train stayed with me forever: 'If I see a Jew, I'll cut his throat here and now,' he hissed at the tram driver. Onkel Mor looked away and motioned for me to follow him off the tram. We walked the rest of the way home. The next day, 9 November, Von Rath died and Hitler instructed his officials to start a pogrom against the Jews. It became known as Kristallnacht.

When the last, and most punitive, of the Nuremberg Laws were implemented, companies were prohibited from employing Jews, who had to give up all their possessions. Even leases were cancelled and you couldn't renew your lease. Property was confiscated, Jews had to take their jewellery to the bank, hand it in, get a receipt, and their bank accounts were closed.

My parents knew their children had no future in the country. Most elderly people stayed because they thought the regime would fail, or their children were already overseas, or were about to leave. We were considered too young to leave on our own. Although my father's boss, Emil Bauer, was given no option but to dismiss him, he demonstrated his decency by trying to help my father set up a subsidiary of the company in Brazil. The plan was that my brother would work in the firm for a couple of months and then go to Brazil after him and start a factory for Hannovera cash registers.

My father had a friend who was also planning to go to Buenos Aires, so my mother went to make some enquiries at a travel agency, where she met a friendly German woman who had already spent time in that city. 'Why would a lady like you go to a place like South America?' the other woman said to her. 'You're a cultured woman – you won't like it there.' My mother was taken aback and pressed her for advice. 'It's a matter of life and death. What would you suggest?'

'For you, Australia,' she replied.

Remembering that her sister Charlotte had married an Australian grazier, my mother took the words to heart and immediately contacted Charlotte. One thing led to another and Onkel Mor, who was very influential in the Berlin Jewish Association, was able to arrange with contacts in Australia to help get the family a landing permit. The family found a benefactor in Sir Samuel Cohen, a prominent businessman and founding president of the Australian Jewish Welfare Society, who said he was prepared to sponsor us. We were desperate to get out but most Jews went to Shanghai, because you didn't need a visa to enter. The problem with Australia was that my father was too old for the migration program. That's why South America seemed attractive. Brazil didn't have an age limit and had already accepted my uncle Heinrich and his wife Gustl. My mother and we two boys went to Australia, but not my father. (There was insufficient time and money for Onkel Mor's application, which ultimately condemned him to take his own life.)

While we struggled to get a permit for Australia, the rest of my family was spread around the globe. My mother's brother and two sisters were still in Germany. The youngest one and her academic husband had moved to South Africa and changed their name. Onkel Heinrich with his wife Gustl were issued a visa for Sao Paolo but he died of a heart attack when he discovered that his was a fake. Aunt Mietze and Onkel Heinrich came to Berlin, thinking they would fare better in a big city than in Mannheim. Instead, they were deported to Auschwitz, allegedly among the first to be gassed. My mother's elder sister Elsa, who had given her life for the German nation in an earlier war, would have been appalled. Charlotte, who was by then safely in Nice, was evacuated to Britain and survived the war there. The Red Cross helped her locate my mother after the war and she moved to Sydney, renting a modest unit in the inner-city suburb of Glebe until her death in 1966.

NEW BEGINNINGS

We left Berlin when it was virtually winter, and the day we arrived in Sydney, less than a week before Christmas 1938, it was over 100 degrees Fahrenheit. 'We can't possibly live here,' my mother declared; she felt the heat more than we did. 'Mum, we've got no option,' I told her. The country's reputation had put us on the lookout for native animals in the streets. We were surprised that there were no kangaroos running around, and we were genuinely disappointed when the locals told us we had to go to the zoo to see them.

After disembarking, we were taken up to the Maccabean Hall, which at the time was a sort of reception centre in Darlinghurst, waiting for the local Jewish Welfare Society to put our lives in order. Instead, nothing happened; we hung around all morning, sweating. In the afternoon we looked around for some accommodation, together with a young, recently married German couple with a newborn baby we met on the ship. They asked my mother if they could live with us to save on rent. She could see a mutual benefit in the idea. So all six of us we went to an apartment block in Clapton Place in Kings Cross, and we took a small two-bedroom unit. The mother would sing her baby to sleep and that's where I learned my first German lullaby, not in Berlin during my own childhood, but in cramped, sweaty Kings Cross when I was fifteen.

We stayed there for only three months, during which time my mother used her dressmaking skills to scrape together money for the rent. Within a week of arriving we were directed to the Toc-H Club in Loftus Street in the city, a servicemen's organisation that provided basic comforts for soldiers and refugees. Here we made our first important contact, Sir Arthur Griffith, the Minister for Public Works, and retired patent attorney. That's the moment Australia became our lucky country.

Sir Arthur was visibly impressed by my mother's courage in tackling a new country with two young boys by herself; he may also have been taken by her good looks. Between the two, he invited us up to his office, and didn't even blink when I sat on and squashed his bowler hat. One thing is indisputable: he went out of his way to give us the best of all starts in our new country. In a letter dated 7 February 1939 Sir Arthur's son, Christian Griffith, confirmed his generosity with this letter:

> Dear Mrs Aram, you will probably remember speaking to me about your sons' education at the Toc-H rooms on Friday night. They are entitled to a free education at the Sydney Boys High School – best school in Sydney – or if they prefer, the Technical High School in Ultimo..
>
> If they will call on my father, he will give them a letter of introduction to the headmaster. Term has already commenced so it would be a good idea for the lads to call on my father as soon as possible.
>
> I know the elder boy [Arnold] is about eighteen but it might be a good idea for him to go to school just the same, even if he only stays a few months until he gets a position.
>
> I shall see you again, probably at the Toc-H rooms, and in the meantime wish you luck in this, your new life.
>
> Yours very sincerely,
>
> Christian Griffith

Sure enough, Sir Arthur secured a job for Arnold at Tullochs Industries as an apprentice welder, and for me a job at David Jones, the department store, as an assistant window dresser, after a medical test in which the dentist told me I needed to have four teeth taken out. When I told my mother, she protested that we didn't have the money. The dentist replied: 'In that case, it's not necessary.' I still have all my teeth.

My brother was paid £2 10s a week as a welder, I earned 17s 6d at David Jones, and my mother, who also worked there, was now earning three or four guineas. Between the three of us we had enough to move out of our cramped apartment in Kings Cross, and my father's impending arrival made this a matter of urgency. My mother spotted a unit on New South Head Road in Rushcutters Bay, down the road from the Cross, for 32s 6d. I vetoed it immediately.

'Mum, I'm not living there; it's too small and noisy,' I blurted. By that stage I was already the choosy one in the family. I called it high standards; the others had less kind words for my sensibility. To compensate for my snobbishness, I went to a real estate agent, who showed us a larger unit on Ocean Avenue in the more elegant suburb of Double Bay, for 38s 6d, which was a big difference in price.

Meanwhile, we took up Sir Arthur's offer of schooling, too, choosing to enrol in night classes at Ultimo Technical College. Arnold studied engineering and I chose bookkeeping. We were well treated by our fellow students, and never felt any discrimination; neither of us spoke with an obvious German accent thanks to having learned English at the American School in Berlin and home studies.

More importantly, Sir Arthur also negotiated a landing permit for my father, despite his age. My mother, organised as ever, had held the £200 landing money in a secure bank account, in anticipation of this very opportunity. The perpetual smile on Sir Arthur's face (which we later learned kept his false teeth in place) prompted my mother to welcome him to our apartment in Ocean Avenue with a beaming salute:

'Sir Arthur, you are always smelling!' He took this as a compliment and smiled even more broadly.

I had an old bicycle which I rode to the city every day for my job at David Jones. The exercise kept me fit and I saved on bus fares. One morning, when I got to the corner of Castlereagh and Park Streets, there was a policeman on point duty (standing on a platform in the intersection). He gave me the signal to turn and as I swung into Castlereagh Street a Rolls-Royce came across against the policeman's signal and knocked me over. Although the bike was absolutely wrecked, I escaped injury. My trousers were torn and I was shaken, but unhurt. I picked myself up and without waiting for the policeman to come over, collected myself and made my way to David Jones with the mangled bike over my shoulder.

When I arrived home in the evening, dishevelled and the worse for wear, my mother admonished me. 'Why didn't you wait for the policeman? Go back and talk to him tomorrow.'

I duly followed this advice and found the policeman, who was again on duty. He smiled. 'Yes, young man, you should have waited, and given me all the details,' he said kindly. The policeman told me the car was at fault and gave me details of the owner. His name was Sir George Julius, a prominent engineer. Sir George was driving next to his chauffeur, who would take the Rolls-Royce home to pick him up in the afternoon.

I made an appointment with Sir George's office and wrote down what my costs were. It came to about £100 for the pants and the bike, which was a lot of money in those days. Sir George was polite and apologetic. After we had finished talking, he rang a bell under his desk, the secretary came in and he said: 'Write this young man a cheque for £100, and a letter that he has no further claims against me.' My eyes lit up. It was my first experience with 'big money'. I opened my first bank account, learned about compound interest and did not touch the money.

Regardless of my accident and the windfall that followed, I was not cut out for working as a window dresser's assistant at David Jones. Whether it was the repetition, the smallness of the tasks, or a teenager distracted by ambition, I stuffed up. One day I was sweeping up the floor before the display was set up when I trod on a mannequin draped in a swimsuit. I trod on its arm and it broke. I draped the swimsuit across the break, hoping no one would notice it – which they didn't, until they cleared the window and it collapsed in a nasty mess.

Another time in the middle of summer there was a window full of nightdresses (perhaps an omen of what was to come). It was very hot, not just from the temperature outside but from the lights in the window itself. To cool off, I took off my dark blue coat, without realising the curtains were already drawn, and put it on one of the nightgowns. This attracted quite a crowd: fingers were pointing at the pink nightdress with a navy blue jacket on.

My biggest mistake came when I was working with heaters in the main display window on the Market Street corner. They ranged in price from £1 to £4. I got the labels mixed up, and a woman came in and insisted on buying the dearer one for just a pound. I knew I was on thin ice and the last straw occurred during the David Jones centenary celebrations. They had a stack of commemorative prints to distribute and I was given a hammer and some nails to hang them up around the store. I remembered that the fourth floor had lots of wooden panels and decided to start hammering there first.

I took four of these advertising handouts, and nailed them onto this polished wood, until the door opened and out came a distinguished-looking man in an elegant suit. 'Young man, these posters are not for the administrative offices,' he said crisply. 'You have to go downstairs.' I had just met Sir Charles Lloyd Jones, the head of the company. Shortly afterwards I received my notice. My salary was due to increase from 17s 6d to 23s and management did not think it was worth their while – and they were right!

Our beloved housekeeper Hedwig, with her husband Willy Knack, in 1949

Stopover in the Canadian Rocky Mountains (November 1938)

A family reunited: my parents and children (Arnold, left, and me) in the garden of our apartment in Manning Road, Double Bay, in 1940, shortly after my father's arrival

A portrait of me in my early twenties

THE EDUCATION OF YOUNG HENRI

I had no job and no prospects but I now had plenty of free time. Like all young boys, I was fascinated with planes and decided to take a tram out to Mascot to inspect the airport, which in those days was very modest. First stop was Mascot Post Office, which was surrounded by paddocks. I walked across the fields where horses and cows were grazing and came to the airport, which consisted of about a dozen hangars.

Around the back a group of men were making wooden aircraft, Tiger Moths, for the Air Force. A light went on in my head at the sight of this gee-whizz technology, which had added importance because of the possibility of war. I wanted to be a part of it, immediately, and promptly walked around to the front, and inside the door of the de Havilland Aircraft company. A lady came out to greet me: 'I would like to know if you have a job vacancy,' I said. 'I don't know,' she replied calmly, 'but I'll get John Mills.'

Out came a mountain of a man – he was about 6 foot 3 inches, and I was about five foot something; my growth spurt had yet to occur. He looked down at me. 'You know, young man, where you have a headache, I have a tummy ache.' While I tried to make sense of his joke, he added more seriously: 'I can't help you because the job appointments are the boss's job – I'm only the engineer, but I'll make a note and I'll let Major

Murray Jones know. He's due back from England and is the head of the business. I'll let him know there's a young man in need of a job.' To his credit, Mr Mills sent me a letter a week or so later advising me to contact Miss Jean Stanger, the Major's secretary, and make an appointment.

At the time I had ambitions to become an architect and had recently received a letter from the leading firm of architects, Turner and Turner, for a second interview. But the thought of building aeroplanes sent a shiver of excitement through me, and with it the courage to ask for a job. A few weeks later, in June 1939, I sat in the de Havilland office with Major Allan Murray Jones. 'You'd have to start in the store and I'd suggest if you want to do well in life, you'll study accountancy,' he advised. 'As part of your salary we'll pay for your accountancy night classes. But there's only one problem. Because you're tiny for your age, we'll have to build a step for you to reach the counter to hand over the spare parts.'

I didn't like being reminded of my height but this was more than compensated by the offer of a job, which I accepted gratefully. It soon became known around de Havilland that I was small for my age and I became known as 'young Henri'. I tried hard to learn all the names of parts in the storeroom, but although my English was fluent I had trouble remembering some of the tools because it was not my mother tongue. One of the workers gave me some homespun advice soon after I started: 'Never run when you can walk; never stand when you can sit; always shit in the bosses' time!' Later, to my embarrassment, some smart alec sent me on a fruitless search for an eight-inch population tool! This language problem was highlighted when one of the other workers came around selling French letters, which I took literally to mean that. I was fifteen, getting on for sixteen, and to me a French 'lettuce' could only be Brussels sprouts.

'Are they nice and fresh?' I asked naively.

'Yes,' he nodded. 'They're a pound a dozen.' This seemed a reasonable price. 'If they are nice and fresh, I'll have a dozen – my mother likes them.' When I actually saw them, I piped up: 'I'm sorry, that's not what I understood it to mean.' The other workers set me straight but it took me a while to live that down. Fortunately, Major Murray Jones and the staff were kind and supportive, and I thrived there.

I had a good job but not much time for leisure, and my mother made no apologies for that. Shortly before his arrival, my father wrote to us: 'Do the kids go swimming?'

'They are too busy working,' she replied bluntly. 'They have no time for swimming.'

We never went to the beach, firstly because, coming from inland Europe it was not a natural form of recreation, and we weren't inclined to spend our spare time getting sand all over us. Also, my parents did not value sport during our formative years back in Berlin. They saw it as time that could have been better spent studying and reading. Even if Arnold and I had been seduced by the sun and sand, we wouldn't have had much time to enjoy it. When the war broke out in September 1939, our liberty was immediately curtailed. We couldn't even leave Double Bay without a permit, let alone frolic on the beach whenever we felt like it.

Around the corner from our apartment was a movie theatre, in New South Head Road, which is where we heard the news that the war had started. A film screening was interrupted to announce the grave news: 'We are now at war with Germany' in the words of Winston Churchill. My brother and I were fired up; he was eighteen and I was sixteen.

'We want to go and fight Hitler,' we announced to our mother, who shook her head defiantly. She needn't have worried. Arnold went to enlist in the army reserve, but before we had time to act on our impulses the government changed our status from refugees to 'enemy aliens'. We never imagined that refugees could be classified as 'enemies'. It was a terrible shock, especially as the loss of our rights and liberties unfolded. We were warned not to speak German because we were now a type of enemy. This was one of the great ironies and injustices: the greatest enemies of the Germans were the Jewish refugees, yet we were regarded by the Australian government as enemy aliens. Officials were concerned about verifying whether new arrivals were genuine refugees. Along the way, mistakes were made – and our family was not immune, as we were soon to find out.

My father arrived in Australia in October 1939, shortly after the outbreak of war, having made his way from Stockholm to Liverpool in England, and from there securing a passage on the *Orontes* to Sydney. At customs the authorities declared him an enemy alien and forced him to hand over a small Box Brownie camera he bought in Ceylon en route to Australia, and a folding camera, an old war souvenir. Some time later a letter arrived from the Customs Department saying that these cameras were of no value and should be collected or they would be destroyed. Despite advice to the contrary, my father chose to collect them. 'They are useless; I am entitled to have them,' he declared.

A few months after, to our shock, he received a summons to Paddington Court on a charge of 'illegal possession of prohibited items' – the two useless cameras. He was confident, as usual – my father always backed himself to overcome adversity – and decided to defend himself. He even welcomed the police when they came to search our house.

'Welcome, come in,' he said.

'We want to search the house,' an officer said.

'Just a moment, I'll go and get my wife,' he replied. My mother came out, and my father promptly went for a walk. He wasn't interested; he just left it to my mother.

The court case was memorable. My father got up and stood in front of the judge, holding the Customs letter as the basis of his defence. Just as he was about to speak, an unknown man rose and told the court he had been instructed by his son to defend my father. My father, stunned at this outburst, retorted that no such instructions had been given; he had a strong case and would defend himself. The magistrate told him to sit down and instructed the solicitor.

My father sat down, alongside his unwanted solicitor. After the guilty sentence, they were approached by a young man with an anxious look.

'Aren't you defending my father?' he said to the solicitor, pointing to the next defendant in the dock.

The solicitor, pointing to my father, replied: 'Isn't this your father?' To which the young man replied: 'I don't know that man!'

The unknown solicitor had got his clients confused and was to offer a defence for a completely different man, a German professor named Moritz Berendt (also from Double Bay) who escaped from Germany to a professorship at Cambridge University before finally settling in Australia. He, too, had been charged with having a camera. My father was suddenly elevated from salesman to professor, without even attending university!

The Sydney *Sun* newspaper had a reporter in the court and published this story:

> On behalf of Julius Aram, Manning Road, Bellevue Hill, it was stated that his son had been a medical student at Berlin University.

> The Gestapo, in 1932, forced the father and son to leave Germany, as they were working for the betterment of Jewish youths.
>
> They were then invited to Cambridge University, and later came to Australia. The son, a linguist, had offered his services to Australia.
>
> Moritz Berendt, Arthur Street, Double Bay, said he thought he could keep his camera so long as he did not use it.

As both men realised what had happened, the bemused magistrate took the easiest option and put the pair of them in the same prison cell, subject to bail. Both were fined £10, a significant amount given their circumstances, and both families refused to pay the solicitor who had ruined both their defences. In the end, my father and Professor Berendt were bailed out by a Reverend Pilcher, a churchman who was a friend of the Berendts and who also helped my mother. Thanks to his generosity, each man slept in his home that night. In hindsight the incident had a comical air, but at the time we were genuinely concerned at what might happen.

The experience, the threat of my father being taken away from me – again – left me with a burning desire to fight injustice. I sat down and wrote the first of hundreds of letters that I would send off over the next 60 years whenever I saw injustice around me. The letter was to the Governor-General, Lord Gowrie, voicing my disappointment with British justice and comparing it to the treatment meted out to innocent people in Germany. To my surprise, the Governor-General replied promptly and generously. He was not allowed to intervene in the jurisdiction of the country, he replied, but enclosed a ten pound note to compensate for my father's fine. This unexpected success imprinted on me the power of letter writing and its strength as a weapon against injustice, no matter whether it was deliberate or accidental.

One crisis was averted and another loomed into view. When the family reunited, our apartment in Ocean Avenue was too small for the four of us. I took it upon myself to scout for something bigger, and spied a first-floor apartment for lease at Manning Road in Double Bay.

I went up to the front door and knocked. An old lady came out. Her name was Mrs Norris and she was followed by her sister, Mrs Herring. I pointed to the sign there for lease. 'How much?' I asked.

'Why do you want to know?' they replied. 'You're a little boy!'

'It's for my parents,' I shot back proudly, blushing slightly.

'It's two guineas.'

'I don't think my parents can pay that.'

Mrs Norris fixed me in the eye: 'You tell your mother to come and see us.'

So my mother came back with me to see Mrs Norris, who was greatly impressed that this little boy had come and knocked on the door. She asked my mother how much she could afford. 'We're paying 38s 6d now.'

'Can you afford to pay two pounds?'

I piped up: 'Yes, of course.'

My mother turned to me: 'How would you know?'

'Of course we can afford two pounds – father is here now.'

Mrs Norris was very impressed and gave us this comfortable upstairs apartment – four bedrooms, but only one bathroom. It was old but there was enough room for my mother to resume her work as a cosmetician.

My father soon landed a job as a door-to-door salesman for a company called Watkins Products, which made washing powders, soap and some oils. He felt comfortable working as a salesman thanks to his experience in Germany. He was confident and direct; people trusted him. During the week he took orders and on Saturdays his two sons tagged along to help deliver them. Once settled into his job, he saw a business opportunity for the family: my mother could start making cosmetics herself; she had the technical knowledge and he had the sales skills. Beauty creams were imported into Australia before the war broke out but the supply dried up once it started. This presented an opening for my mother: one of her clients was married to a Hungarian industrial chemist, Dr Andrew Unger, who (among other achievements) invented Andrews Liver Salts, which may still be manufactured today. Dr Unger also had a formula for a marvellous face cream. He gave my mother the recipe and she had room enough in the house at our Manning Road apartment to store industrial compounds in the back room and kitchen. My father would go around with a suitcase of her creams and lotions, selling them in the same way as he did for Watkins. Before long they had about half a dozen people selling the cosmetics for them. The business did quite well, and they were able to rent a room in an arcade in Rose Bay at the shopping centre where Newcastle Street runs into New South Head Road.

Some time later, my parents went on holiday and left the cosmetics business in our care for a while. My mother showed my brother and me how to make the face creams. We ran out of stock already made, and decided to make our own. Instead of using the prescribed correct chemicals, we used one of the ingredients designated for a face mask, which contained a skin stimulant that expanded the mixture. We left the jars overnight and returned to see the lids broken. What did we know? We thought we had filled them too tightly, so we skimmed it off, and made another dozen jars. When my mother came back, she was horrified and raced around to tell her clients what had happened. Fortunately it did no harm, but it was a money spinner. In those days, my mother sold her jars for 2s – it was a lot of money.

In 1940 the Battle of Britain began in earnest and life for foreigners in Australia, which was already heavily restricted, deteriorated severely. Security police came around to round up and intern all 'enemy aliens' who were working at de Havilland and I was only saved by the intervention of Major Murray Jones, who sent his solicitor to court to plead a special case for me. 'This young man is under the supervision of the head of the company,' the solicitor declared to the judge, and claimed I was important for the war effort because I had introduced the Dewey decimal system into the Tiger Moth warehouse, having learned about it in my night studies. The Dewey system was a numerical system of ordering used by libraries, and I applied it to aeroplane parts. I knew all the part numbers off by heart, and within a year I could tell anyone where they were. The solicitor argued persuasively and my case was upheld.

By day I worked for de Havilland, at night I studied accountancy at a correspondence education company, Hemmingway and Robertson, paid for by the firm. You did their courses at home at night, and later sat for the exams. I enjoyed the challenge, learned quickly, and the next year I was ready for my first exam. . However, unlike the other students, I was not allowed to sit for it because I was an enemy alien.

With the success of my letter to the Governor-General still fresh in my mind, I decided to write to Doctor H.V. Evatt, the Attorney-General and Minister for External Affairs in the new Labor Government. 'This discrimination was exactly what we experienced in Germany, and we thought the British would be different,' I wrote. Once again, a government official took me seriously. Dr Evatt replied and put a stop to it. I was starting to see that a well-argued case could get you somewhere in this country.

When I finally qualified, the Association of Accountants wouldn't register me as a member. A Mr Williams from the International Institute of Accountants came to my aid: 'Of course, we'll have you,' he wrote to me. (Years later, his grand-daughter happened to come into my practice one day. She saw my signed certificate of membership. 'The man who signed this was my grandfather,' she said. 'My grandfather must have motioned me from heaven that I must get in touch with you.')

In time I was promoted to Planning Officer for both Tiger Moth and Mosquito aircraft, which were built out at Bankstown, in Sydney's west. At that time there were only two flights a week interstate and perhaps one a week from overseas. That meant the airport runways were pretty clear most of the time, and that's where I learned to drive – in Archie Steinbeck's petrol wagon. It was a terrific place to learn, with no traffic to worry about. Actually, the main hazard was the occasional crash of the Tiger Moths that whirred past us from time to time. The most memorable of these was the time Nancy Bird Walton, the famous aviator, misjudged a landing and flipped her Tiger Moth in the swamp surrounding the airport. As we rushed out on Archie's wagon to see what had happened and whether the pilot was hurt, we were greeted by a sight I shall never forget. There was Nancy Bird, nonchalant as ever, sitting on the edge of the plane, smiling and knitting while she waited for us to bring her back to base.

I had an even closer brush with fate soon after that, thanks to a suggestion to Major Murray Jones one day that future aircraft should be powered by propulsion rather than the conventional pull of propellers. He turned to me with a startled look on his face. 'They are working on this in Britain and it is top secret,' he whispered. In view of my interest and keen mind, the major arranged for me to go on a test flight of a locally produced Mosquito. At the last minute, however, I agreed to make room for a visiting engineer from Melbourne. It proved to be one of my best decisions. The plane disintegrated over Petersham in the inner suburbs of Sydney and both occupants died.

While we had relative material comfort, our movements were still curtailed because of wartime restrictions. As enemy aliens we couldn't go out at night after 7 pm. There was a curfew and there were blackouts. Air raid wardens shone powerful spotlights through the windows. Although these rules applied to everyone, the pressure was worse for us because people were suspicious. My mother, with the memories of Nazism fresh in her mind, was paranoid that neighbours would accuse us of signalling to boats off the coast. We needed a travel permit just to go to the city, which was renewable with the Rose Bay police every week. If you tried to travel without a permit, it caused problems. I remember taking a girl to the Tivoli Theatre, in the city precinct. My travel permit was to Mascot, but I didn't have a travel permit to go to the City on a Saturday night. We took the risk. I bought her some Jaffas, and she opened them as the curtain went up. Everything was quiet, and she dropped the whole bloody box. All the Jaffas rolled down the wooden stairs. I was horrified that someone would come up, ask me for my papers and discover that I didn't have a travel permit.

As the Nazis drew closer to defeat, the Australian government relaxed its regulations and 'enemy aliens' were reclassified as 'friendly enemy aliens'. We were grateful for the change of status: travel restrictions were eased, we could apply for a driver's licence (although we didn't yet have a car). Towards the end of the war, Arnold and I were invited to a New Year's Eve party in Burwood with two girls. On the far side of the city, we missed the last train home. We walked along Parramatta Road until a police car picked up the two girls. Arnold and I had to walk for another two hours until a newspaper delivery truck gave us a ride; we arrived home at dawn. My mother, who was always melancholy at this time of year – her birthday and the anniversary of her mother's death – was in a state of high anxiety when she set eyes on us.

The new year brought a health scare for me, the first of many. After a routine check-up, a Macquarie Street specialist misdiagnosed my heart palpitations – from anxiety about being at the doctor's – as congenital heart disease and recommended an immediate removal of my tonsils. When my mother suggested a second opinion after such unexpected news, his reply was: 'Hitler was unexpected, too.' The two other doctors had good and bad news: my heart would never get better as there was nothing wrong with it, and the ENT specialist found my tonsils not in great condition but in no need of removal.

When the war ended in 1945, and we were able to get our drivers' licences, my brother bought an Austin, and I bought an old Vauxhall, so we each had a car. My mother was horrified that people would see that we had two cars in the family. Most people didn't have one car, let alone two, and she thought we would look too conspicuous. She was still anxious about our status.

While Arnold and I enjoyed the freedom that young men crave from cars, my father looked to simpler pleasures in his spare time. Now nearly 70 years old, he loved to walk a lot, as he used to do in Berlin, and enjoyed sauntering up to Kings Cross, which in those days had some of the Bohemian nightlife that he remembered in the old country. For something special, he would often pack a case with books, take a train to Katoomba in the Blue Mountains by himself and book into the Palais Royale, a fashionable hotel and a favoured haunt of European migrants.

For her part, my mother still lived frugally. She would go to Taylor

Square in Darlinghurst, where there were many migrant shops, to buy chicken giblets. The shops gave them away if you bought half a pound of chicken fat. So she bought the chicken fat, and took the giblets home. My mother would make schmaltz, as a butter substitute, and we would have a week's meat. Old habits died hard. However, I was cut from a different cloth. I bought my first suit down at Haymarket for a couple of pounds and my mother thought I was extravagant.

A lot of soldiers now returned home looking for jobs. I went to Major Murray Jones: 'I don't think it's fair for me to take a job of a returned soldier, and I think I should vacate my position for somebody coming back from the war.' Though surprised at my self-sacrifice, the Major clearly appreciated my gesture and the company sent me a letter of appreciation. He and I became firm friends and a few years later, when I started my business, he drove out with his chauffeur to look at my factory at Auburn. He was impressed and invited me to the Royal Sydney Golf Club for lunch, and we remained in touch for many years. When I left de Havilland in 1945, they gave me an excellent reference:

> Henri Aram … showed outstanding ability and readily grasped the details of his work … During the period of Mr Aram's employment with us, he obtained our advice as to how he could best spend his leisure time in the evening and on our recommendation, took a course of Accountancy and prior to leaving us was, I believe, on the point of taking his final examination …
>
> We always found him to be a most conscientious young man of excellent character and ability. He was always most courteous and

> willing and I am sure he will enjoy a successful future, in connection with which he has our very best wishes.

I used my new found freedom to finish my accounting studies by day at the State Library (and was made a member of the Australian Association of Accountants). I also met a young girl, Ilse, who was studying there, and we went out a few times. I enjoyed having a social life, and more time to myself, having worked so hard during my late teenage years. But that relationship was interrupted by another, the unexpected meeting with a middle-aged man. Opportunity was about to knock again, very loudly, and all because I was a dutiful son.

MATERIAL BENEFITS

His name was Mr Epstein – I didn't know his first name at the time – and he was an American-born industrialist who lived alone in Rosemont, an elegant apartment block on Edgecliff Road in Woollahra, one of Sydney's most exclusive addresses. Mr Epstein owned and ran a textile company called Silknit. Rosemont residents routinely employed housekeepers to help them. Mr Epstein's housekeeper was a German woman named Ms Wills (not Jewish), who had been victimised after an affair with a Jewish man in Germany. She was considered guilty of 'shaming her race' and more or less forced to leave the country. Her lover went to Cuba and he was to arrange for her to go there when the war intervened. She found a job as Epstein's housekeeper and became friends with my mother through her cosmetics business.

At Christmas in 1945, Mr Epstein invited his housekeeper to throw a party for her friends. 'I'm going to Melbourne, I won't be back till later in the week.' The housekeeper invited my mother on a Friday and I picked her up from the party as Mr Epstein was returning home. 'Who was that young man?' Mr Epstein asked his housekeeper after seeing me coming out. When she explained who I was, he continued: 'What does he do?' She found out I studied accountancy and told him. He told her to get me to contact his secretary. 'I'd like to have a chat with him.'

A few days later I put on some smart clothes and made my way to the Silknit office, near Central Station, where many of the clothes manufacturing and textile businesses were clustered. The housekeeper had mentioned that he might have a job for me, which whetted my appetite. I had nothing lined up because I wanted to finish my accountancy degree; I still had ambitions about architecture, too.

Mr Epstein's office was large and commanding. After we exchanged pleasantries, he opened his drawer and pulled out a photo. 'That's my son in his army uniform. Don't you think he looks like you?' he said quietly. I nodded at the likeness. 'Yes, he does.'

His son, who was around my age, was a lieutenant in the US Army. 'I asked him to come to Australia and he didn't want to come.' He looked at me straight in the face. 'I've been checking up on you. You've studied accountancy, you've worked for six years. You have the qualifications I would want from my eventual successor. Would you care to join this business if I promised to teach you all there is to know?'

It seemed hard to believe what I had just heard and I stopped for a moment to reflect. A friendly stranger wanted to groom me to take over his company because I looked like his absent son. But what did I know about Mr Epstein or his business? I knew he was rich because I had seen his home, and his office. But beyond that … I didn't know if he was a widower, or whether his wife was with his son in America. In fact, I didn't know whether he was telling me the truth about his background at all, but felt I could trust his intentions. At that stage I didn't even know his first name – he was just Mr Epstein. But I had always liked a challenge, and when opportunity knocks you answer. My parents were keen.

'What have you got to lose?' my father said.

'He likes you and promised to teach you the business. That's half the battle,' my mother said.

It was an offer too good to refuse. And that is how I started in the textile industry.

Mr Morris Epstein promised to take me through all the various processes – manufacture, knitting, dyeing, design, cutting. Thanks to this thorough grounding in the physical skills of textile work, when I finally started my own business I knew how to talk, order, cut and stand as an equal with various suppliers and merchants who tried to take advantage of me. I had a favoured status at Silknit because of my likeness to his son. In a way, Mr Epstein treated me as a substitute for him. Although he was quiet, somewhat reticent, the other workers could see there was something special about our relationship. I worked hard and learned quickly. However, he kept our relationship strictly professional. I was never invited to his home for dinner, I never met his son. Indeed, Mr Epstein never again spoke to me about his son.

The business was prospering and Mr Epstein decided to expand; he wanted to open a factory in South Africa and suggested I go over and help set it up. I was reluctant. My parents thought the opportunities for work were better here in Australia, and I didn't particularly want to leave my family behind. However, I wasn't yet ready to step into Mr Epstein's shoes in Australia so he appointed a very intimidating man called Trinidad, a staunch Catholic in his mid-forties, to take over. The production manager was a Mr Saltzman, who took me under his wing and taught me everything he knew about cutting. I had an affinity for the technical side of the work, as well as the business, and enjoyed the intricacies of how fabric could be used in different ways for particular types of garments.

I never knew whether Mr Epstein had given Saltzman, a Canadian Jew, specific instructions to take care of me. But his kindness was trumped by the behaviour of Trinidad, who made my life very hard, harder than it should be. With Mr Epstein out of the picture, Trinidad was free to express himself. It became clear that he didn't like me, he felt threatened by my special status with Mr Epstein. Trinidad excluded me from all the executive functions that Mr Epstein had wanted me to experience and learn. There was no future for me at Silknit under him.

One of our clients was a certain Frank Tieman from the women's underwear company Osti. Tieman was a Viennese Jew who had been an underwear salesman in his homeland. Shortly before the war, he and his wife caught a boat from Europe to escape the trouble and on board they met an Australian couple, the O'Sullivans, coming back from a trip to Europe. The O'Sullivans and Tiemans played bridge together on the cruise and struck up a friendship. O'Sullivan was a wealthy grazier. 'Come to Australia!' he invited Tieman, 'and start an underwear business here. I tell you what. If you come to Australia, I will finance you.' Tieman could smell a good offer when he saw one. And that's how the Osti company was born. The first two letters of O'Sullivan and Tieman.

Although Tieman had sold underwear for a long time, he didn't have a clue how to make it and largely relied on his mother-in-law to help him. Whenever he placed an order with me, he asked me to mark out all his layers for months ahead. When I obliged, and did it accurately, he was impressed. 'Would you like to join me at Osti?' he asked one day. 'No, thanks,' I told him firmly. 'I am happy where I am.' Tieman was small, noisy, jovial and could be quite aggressive. I didn't particularly want to work for him. That would prove to be one of my better business decisions, in view of his later career in property development.

Tieman did not take my rejection personally. In fact, I must give him credit for advancing my career when I left Silknit in 1946 thanks to Mr Trinidad's bullying. Through the lingerie business, Tieman was friends with another manufacturer called Emery Strasser, a Hungarian who ran a textile company called Emstra (named after his first two names, Em Stra).

Strasser was looking for skilled young workers who spoke good English. One day Tieman told Strasser about this young man who had worked at Silknit. A look of awakening shot over Strasser's face. 'My daughter Ilse knows him from the State Library,' he exclaimed. Strasser called me in, thinking he could kill two birds with one stone – a new manager and a son-in-law all in one. 'I need somebody to take over my business,' he told me, just as Morris Epstein had done a couple of years earlier. I joined up on his promise, because I now had my accountancy degree and I knew the industry. It was less than a year since I had left Silknit.

As assistant general manager at Emstra, my responsibilities included not just manufacture and retail but also ensuring we negotiated good deals on material and dyes. At some point, a dye and bleach company in Newtown (called Newtown Dyers and Bleachers) came onto the market. Emstra and Osti thought it would be a good idea to buy the dye house together for their respective companies. This brought me back into contact with Frank Tieman (who had changed his name to Theeman) and it was my duty to negotiate with him about what we would pay for the dye house. Theeman's swearing and aggression raised my antennae; I kept our relationship strictly business.

Emstra soon started to manufacture nylon, which was a very scarce commodity, and our insurance company insisted we employ a night watchman to make sure nobody tried to steal it. It was suggested that we find a stoker for the dye house, someone who stokes the furnace to heat the dye vats, who could double up as a night watchman. Stokers usually came from ships, where they had learned the trade. Soon enough, we found a sailor who performed the two roles for us. The nylon material was sewn together in one huge long constant roll which went through the dyeing process.

One night the watchman decided to nick off early to the local pub, where he got drunk with some old sailing cronies. In his stupor, he hatched a plan to steal some of our material. 'I work in this factory, we'll get a taxi, and take a couple of rolls of nylon and we'll set ourselves up,' he told his mates. So they drove to the factory and let themselves in, but because he was so drunk he forgot to switch off the alarm that let security know he'd returned.

They took what they thought was one roll, put it into the boot of the taxi, not realising that there were another ten rolls inside, which now anchored the material to the dye house. By the time the security guards turned up, there was one continuous roll stretching from the taxi to the factory! It must have been 2 am when I got the call to come and identify them. As a result of the fiasco, the company lost faith in the dye house manager, a man called Wilkes, and decided he had to be sacked. Strasser told me to go with Theeman to break the news to him.

It was not unusual for the two of us to go see him together, as both companies had joint ownership of the dye house. We sat in the office while Wilkes took a phone call. As we waited, Theeman turned to me with a glint in his eye, put his hand in his pocket and pulled out a gun. 'Just in case,' he said to me in a low voice. I was so shocked I couldn't speak. Fortunately, he had no reason to use it. We gave Wilkes the sack, he took it civilly and the encounter proceeded without incident. As we walked back down the road, silently, it dawned on me that Theeman was prepared to involve me in a crime, without any warning.

I didn't know he carried a gun and I was so distressed that I went straight to Strasser. 'Never again will I have anything to do with Frank Theeman,' I told him. Strasser didn't blink when I told him what happened. He knew what sort of person Theeman was. They grew up in business in the Austro-Hungarian Empire. People did business differently over there. Certainly, Theeman's action was an omen of things to come. He resorted to strong-arm tactics more frequently later in his career, after he sold Osti to the Dunlop company in 1972 and moved into property development. He became a central figure in the Kings Cross development battles of the early 1970s, was named in the investigation into the disappearance of activist Juanita Nielsen and his actions helped lead to the union-instigated Green Bans in 1972.

THE BOSS'S DAUGHTER

It's an old cliché that you should never get involved with the boss's daughter. But I wasn't old; I was 23 when I met Ilse Strasser, and she was a little younger. At first we were just friends, two young people who studied together at the library. I did not have many girlfriends before meeting her; I was too busy working and trying to make my way in the world. Our friendship grew and soon something clicked between us. Ilse was quiet and attractive, she had an intellectual air about her. After a couple of years, our relationship became serious. I was not a big talker and our engagement was understated, to put it mildly. Basically, I went and asked Ilse's father for permission to marry her. Emery Strasser was quietly spoken, like his daughter, but his feelings about me were clear. I was a good match for his daughter, with the bonus of being a possible successor to his company. His wife, Irene, was keen on the marriage but less excited about my role in the business. She wanted their son, Eric, at that time just thirteen, to eventually fill his father's shoes.

My parents were not as keen on the marriage, and expressed their reservations from the start. It wasn't just the speed of our engagement, or my youth – my father had not married until his forties and thought that men needed to be better established before they settled down. His other concern was about my financial dependence on my boss. While I learned the ropes and rose through his company, Strasser paid me out of the company earnings. 'You must get an independent, formal contract,' my father insisted. 'You must know where your money is coming from. Otherwise, you are hostage to your father-in-law's goodwill. Anything that happens in your private life could affect your income, and you will have no recourse.'

'I will go and formalise my salary,' I pacified him, without really seeing the point. In the flush of youth, and my awkward situation, I did not heed his words, but I soon understood the reason for his misgivings.

For our engagement, I bought Ilse a large diamond ring from a prominent jeweller, Leo Steiner, in the city. I paid £600 for it – a huge amount of money for someone of my age and in my situation – and was bursting with pride when I handed it to her. 'It's lovely,' she beamed at me. I could tell Ilse was very happy, in her own modest way, and allowed myself a little smile. Ilse showed it proudly to her parents; she was particularly keen for her father's endorsement as she was quite clearly attached to him.

'Look at the engagement ring Henri gave me, Father.'

Strasser took his time inspecting it. 'Nice ... but it has a slightly yellow tinge,' he said when he held it up to his eye.

'Where did you buy it?' he said. When I told him the name of the jeweller, he trampled over what was left of my ego. 'Yes, I know him. I will go and talk to the jeweller and get him to change it for a pure white diamond stone,' he announced nonchalantly. And that was it. No opportunity for me to say or do anything. I was gobsmacked but caught between a rock and a hard place: my fiancée's finger and my boss's authority. My own father's words started ringing in my head.

The next few weeks with Ilse were awkward, to say the least. The ring cast a shadow over what should have been a happy time for us. I didn't know what to say to her, and she was too embarrassed to raise the subject with me. Sure enough, her father called us in one day to show us the ring with a different stone – a white diamond. He handed it to Ilse, who admired its gleam like the dutiful daughter she was.

'Now, that's a beautiful ring,' Strasser said quietly. Ilse went over to hug her father. I let the insult slide past, but then came the injury.

'Now, about the price. This new stone cost two thousand pounds,' my future father-in-law revealed. 'Whenever you've got the time, can you go down and pay the jeweller the difference between this and the first stone? There's no rush but we don't want him to be out of pocket for long.'

The colour drained from my face and I looked at Ilse, too shocked, and compromised, to speak up. I was scared to tell my parents. My father was almost snarling, a very rare sight. 'Just tell him you haven't got the money,' he said. 'You have to be blunt with this man. He has too much control over you.'

My father was right again but I couldn't bring myself to do it. I paid the money, my parents were outraged and my relationship with the Strassers soured from that moment on. In hindsight, this should have been the beginning of the end of the engagement. But it wasn't. I should have seen what this told me about my future. But I didn't. I was young, I thought these sorts of problems, family tensions and friction, were par for the course for every impending marriage.

The wedding was held at the Temple Emmanuel in Woollahra, in 1949, a little over two years after Ilse and I met. It was solemnised by Rabbi Rudolph Brasch, who later became famous as the author of several books on folklore and the origin of customs. Our family first met him in Berlin. I had a cousin who wanted to become a rabbi; his name was Franz Rosenthal, who had met Rabbi Brasch in rabbinical college. When my cousin came for a visit, he brought Rabbi Brasch along with him. In our home in Berlin, Rabbi Brasch spoke perfect German. Now, when he came to our house in Sydney ahead of the wedding, he wouldn't speak German with my father; he would only speak English. My father wasn't impressed.

However, the wedding was a happy event. Ilse looked beautiful, her parents beamed with pride and I told myself the earlier friction was just part of the pre-wedding jitters. My parents put on a smiling face, as my father looked on the bright side. I was young, I had a beautiful wife and good prospects. For our honeymoon, Ilse and I headed to Europe for six weeks. First a cruise, then the Isle of Capri in Italy, followed by London, France and Sweden – a mixture of sightseeing and catching up with family. On the cruise we sat at the same dining table as Norman Smorgon, patriarch of the meat processing and steel dynasty from Melbourne, and his wife. We became friendly and Norman decided to provide Ilse and me with the finance to buy an Austin 40 car for our tour around Europe. 'You pay me back when you get home,' he said. He also invited me to come and work for his company, which was just starting to move into wholesale meat processing. 'When you get back to Australia, go and see my son, Victor,' he said. I was flattered but already in a complicated family business and didn't fancy making my life harder by getting involved with another one.

After we had left the cruise we went to Nice to visit my Aunt Charlotte, who settled there after the war, and again meet Smorgon, who had arranged to see us there. He had broken his arm in a car accident, having run his Humber under a truck after forgetting which side of the road to drive on. Because he was at fault in the accident, the French police made him stay in France until the insurance was processed and paid. I stayed in Nice to help him deal with the police, the car and the insurance claim.

(Fifty years later, in 2001, I sent Victor a letter recalling my encounters with his father. Victor replied: 'The meeting you had with my father and uncle some 50 years ago has brought back a lot of memories for me. In fact, I have a picture of my father, stepmother, uncle and aunt, all bandaged up following the accident that you mention in your letter. I am enclosing a copy of that picture for you ... Thank you for remembering my father and, even if it has taken 50 years to deliver his message, it is very much appreciated.')

On our return to Sydney, Ilse and I moved to a house in Castlecrag on the North Shore. The house was beautifully built on one of the many cliffs in the suburb, and it had a gorgeous view of Middle Harbour. Ilse settled down to married life and I went back to work with my (now) father-in-law. However, being married to the boss's daughter would prove to be far more complicated than I could have ever imagined. The engagement ring saga was child's play compared to what happened next.

In 1950, just one year after we were married, Emery Strasser took ill and asked me to take over the business. My father-in-law was diagnosed with serious stomach cancer. Doctors here told him his best chance of beating it would be at the Mayo Clinic in the US. At the age of 27, I was thrust into the role of chief executive officer of a business that consisted of production and manufacturing in Sydney and Junee, in central western NSW, knitting mills in Petersham and the dye house in Newtown. We also had a number of retail shops, in Kings Cross and Bondi Junction. I was now loaded with all of these responsibilities to run on my own, with about 200 employees in total.

The Strassers were desperate to get treatment and immediately made plans to fly to the Mayo Clinic (Mr Strasser complained to me, in private, that his wife had packed a black mourning outfit, complete with all the trimmings, for the trip). The Mayo Clinic doctors diagnosed that the cancer was inoperable and advised him to return to Sydney to spend the rest of his time in the bosom of his family. While making arrangements to return, they were told of an American surgeon pioneering a radical type of surgery. They went to see him straight away.

'Look, I can operate. You've got a 30 per cent chance but I can't guarantee better than that,' he told them. They took the risk, he operated, and it was successful. So about six months after the treatment, he returned to Sydney, accompanied by the American doctor to oversee his recovery. By the time Emery recovered sufficiently to take over the reins again, I had been running things for about two years. During this period, I faced unexpected hurdles, largely due to his teenage son, Eric, who was just seventeen when his father took leave from the business. The plane had hardly taken off when Eric installed himself in his father's office, changed his name from Eric George to Eric Michael, so his initials would be EM and fit with the Emstra company name, and put his father's photographs on the desk. Egged on privately by his mother, he thought he was running the show.

Straight away he caused trouble for me. While working at Emstra I had saved a bit of money after paying off the diamond ring and ordered a Jaguar car as an investment, with the idea of reselling it for a profit. Jaguars were scarce at that time and there was a year's waiting list to get one. I took delivery of the car while Strasser was away in America and paid for it with my own money, using a personal cheque. It has always been my policy in life never to write a cheque from any firm's account. I always got somebody else – the secretary or accountants – to write the cheques.

One night Ilse and I invited Eric to dinner at our Castlecrag home. The Jaguar, a beautiful dark grey, was too long for our garage and stuck out into the driveway. Eric noticed the car and was impressed. In those days you could make a few hundred by onselling a luxury car.

I advertised it for sale and one of the first people to inspect the car was a Mr Minter, whose father helped found the law firm Minter Simpson (later Minter Ellison). Minter brought his father along to see the car. The older man loved it and bought it. I had not driven the car and I made a tidy profit on the sale.

Meanwhile, Eric had secretly instructed the company accountants to check the books to see if any money had been taken out to pay for the car. Naturally, he didn't find anything but I was incensed that he thought I might be dishonest, and that he would stoop to spying on me to get rid of me.

When Strasser and his wife returned from America, I told him how unhappy I was at Eric's behaviour. Emery was understanding but Irene was keen for Eric to come into the business and started working on Ilse. Ultimately, they turned her against me and ruined the marriage. It was a nasty divorce because everyone had something to say, and Irene was a nasty person. (Ironically, she died before Emery. He remarried a year or two afterwards.) I left Emstra in October 1952; Ilse and I were divorced a year later, in November 1953. She later married a Polish Holocaust survivor, they had two children and went to live in America and Israel. She now lives in New Mexico, but returns to Sydney occasionally. Despite misgivings on my part, I agreed to have coffee with her at our original meeting place, the State Library – which was arranged by my present wife, Robin.

MINDING MY OWN BUSINESS

My mother was devastated by my divorce, my father seemed to expect it. I got over the pain the best way I knew how – by throwing myself into my work. I gave Emstra three months' notice and during these three months I created my own company, A.R.A.M. Industries, with an operating subsidiary known as Auburn Rayon Apparel Mills (ARAM). Throughout my business life, my four-letter surname has always stood me in good stead. When it became known in the trade that I had resigned, customers came to me, the bank offered to help and suppliers said they would support me, so I was encouraged to start on my own, something I had never intended to do. But the opportunities were there. I saw a niche in children's underwear and nightwear, which also used less material, although the labour costs were the same.

During this three-month period, David Jones indicated it would support me, and Fosseys also made positive noises. I was fortunate in that I had a friend, a real estate agent named Des Eady, who I met when I was still working at Emstra. The company needed a new factory premises and Des suggested a block of land opposite the station in Rawson Street, Auburn. Emstra took an option over block but eventually bought land instead at Regents Park, then engaged the famous architect Harry Seidler to design a factory for the site; it was never built due to a family feud. (Seidler was, in fact, friendly with my first wife Ilse, so I knew him socially in the early days. We were in the same circle, although then he became famous and married into the Evatt family.) I later bought the block in Rawson Street myself and sold it to help finance my property holdings.

Des Eady found me a perfect spot for my new factory: a community hall in Auburn, near Parramatta in Sydney's western suburbs, that was intended for use by old-age pensioners but rented to a children's cuddle-seat manufacturer. This property was a wooden structure and the agent said some of the cutting tables and machine could stay there as it was a bankruptcy sale. After we negotiated the purchase, it turned out that a lot of the staff from Emstra lived in the suburb of Auburn. In those days it took a good 45 minutes to travel from Auburn to the city. So I had a ready-made workforce, if I could tap into it. Unbeknown to me, the forewoman had put a notice up on the toilet doors at the Emstra factory, saying: 'Aram is now at Auburn, and you should apply for a job.' The forewoman lived round the corner from my new place and could see the benefits. A lot of the Emstra girls could see them, too. I had been popular with the staff and within weeks, 30 girls applied for jobs.

By the end of 1953, within the three months' notice period, my business was up and running. In anticipation of a reaction from Osti and Emstra, I told my bank manager I wanted to subcontract my material rather than use an existing supplier such as Stirling Henry, which supplied Emstra and Osti with their raw material; this would have left me vulnerable to commercial pressure from them. With my bank manager's approval, I imported my own yarn, and the bank gave me an overdraft of £30,000 (secured by a second mortgage on my Rose Bay home) – a huge amount for a self-starter in those days.

The bank manager, Mr Morton, was a returned soldier. 'Look, Henri, in my 30 years with the bank, I've never lost it a cent. Don't break my record.'

'Mr Morton, you won't lose the money,' I reassured him.

I worked from five o'clock in the morning, sending the knitting to a subcontractor in Parramatta Road, and I repaid the whole loan. My instinct about the opposition was vindicated. Both Emstra and Osti told Stirling Henry not to supply me with material, which in fact alerted the company to the fact that I was now on my own. They contacted me and offered to supply me. Before long I employed close to 50 young girls in the factory, many of them recruited by my old forelady.

I had taken Ilse to Stockholm on our honeymoon to meet the family on my father's side, Erik and Gladys Wolff, and his brother Torston. Gladys came from a very well-known family, the Traugotts, prominent in business and the arts. Her father Ivan, through his business contacts, was an ardent collector of antique jades, a hobby he shared with King Gustaf of Sweden, and resulted in a friendship between them (the Traugott collection was left to the State on his death and is now in the National Museum).

He was also a major shareholder in one of Sweden's largest department stores, which held the franchise to a novel type of packaged furniture made from birchwood, which had just been released there. Through his intervention, I was given the production rights for this furniture in Australia and provided with all drawings and assistance.

On my return I started the venture in a small factory as an adjunct to my textile interests but the local coachwood proved no match for the superior European birch and the business faltered. However, among the carpenters I hired was a Jewish Polish machinist who had built billiard tables before he fled the regime.

The man's name was Dienstag but he called himself Dean. One day, when I came to the factory, I was told he had been called away because his wife had a serious accident. They lived in Rose Bay on busy New South Head Road. She had tried to jump on a moving tram from the wrong side and was rolled under the tram.

'How bad is she?' I asked the foreman.

'We don't know, but she's badly injured and has to have an operation,' he replied.

I was shocked and some days later went to the hospital, St Vincent's in Darlinghurst. There was Mr Dean with his pretty young daughter.

The operation did not go smoothly. His wife was delirious and had thrown a wash basin at a nurse, prompting the doctors to commit her to a mental hospital as they could not keep her there. Then the full story unfolded. Mrs Dean had seen a cross – St Vincent's was a Catholic hospital – and remembered her sufferings under the Nazis and now thought it was a concentration camp.

The doctors wanted to commit her to Gladesville mental hospital. 'Either you take her out, or we commit her to Gladesville,' the doctor warned.

I said to Mr Dean: 'If I were you, I would not commit her to the mental hospital. I would take her home and get a second opinion.' He took my advice and in the meantime used his carpentry skills to make a special bed to keep her leg up. I found a specialist through my mother, a Dr Hertz. He was honest: 'Look, this woman can never walk, because after the operation she has one leg shorter than the other and she needs another operation.' Mr Dean couldn't afford it.

'Leave that to me,' I replied. 'She had been on her way to work when it happened, so she'll have insurance. Get a solicitor.'

She had another operation, and lo and behold, after a few months in a wheelchair she could walk. It left a small mark on her leg but that was nothing compared to what she had faced beforehand. Meanwhile, the expenses were mounting up. It so happened that the insurance company of my firm was the same company that covered her employer. 'Could you help me?' I asked my insurance agent.

'The accident was self-inflicted and the insurance company will not cover her,' he said bluntly.

'But leave it to me,' he said.

So we arranged through the solicitor that we would claim £50,000 damages. We knew we had no case, but when it came to court the insurance company said they wanted to settle and offered £10,000.

Mr Dean said: 'I would have to think that over.'

'Mr Dean, you don't have to think it over. You have no case,' I explained. 'We will settle,' I told the solicitor. We settled all the expenses, Mrs Dean became a very good friend, and they thought maybe I could marry her daughter. They knew my own marriage had ended and having seen how I helped them, and that I had some money, thought I might be a good catch.

After our divorce, Ilse returned to the family home, I left our house in Castlecrag and had used my savings to buy a house for my parents in Rose Bay, one suburb along from the flat they had in Double Bay. I lived there with them. I was 30 years old. However, the daily commute to my new premises in Auburn started taking its toll and my mother declared it was too far for me to go from Rose Bay every day to Auburn. I would leave at five in the morning, and get home at nine or ten at night. In 1954, a year or so after starting my business at Auburn, I gave in to her complaints and bought a property at Strathfield, in the inner west, negotiated by Des Eady. It was handy to my business but still close enough to the city thanks to excellent rail connections.

Soon after we moved into Strathfield, my father broke his hip and we needed a permanent live-in carer/housekeeper. At first we tried to get an Aboriginal girl supplied by the Aboriginal Council. But the Aboriginal Council didn't think it was right for a young girl to move into a house where a young single man lived – even if I was with my parents.

We were directed to the German Consulate, which had a steady stream of migrants looking for housework. The staff told us about a girl from Germany who was very capable but who unfortunately had an illegitimate child. This woman had not coped well with her situation and ended up in Callan Park, a mental institution in Ryde, but was ready for discharge if we wanted to take the risk. My mother and I went to Callan Park to interview this woman, named Karen. My mother was impressed with her. 'We'll give her a go,' she said cheerfully.

'What do you think?' she asked me.

'I think it'll be alright,' I nodded. So we signed her out, taking full responsibility. She fitted in well and did a very good job. (My mother, concerned the girl might try to take advantage of a single, young man, fitted a locking bolt inside the door of my bedroom!)

As fate would have it, we also had a German electrician, who came to do some work late one afternoon. My mother invited him to stay for dinner; Karen came in and served the dishes. On the way in and out, she overheard him telling us a story: 'You're so lucky to have a German girl. I have a customer at Dover Heights [in the Eastern Suburbs]. He got a girl from Germany, straight off the ship. She was very good, but she was pregnant, and she gave birth to a child. I don't know what happened to her since then.'

Next morning, Karen wouldn't come out of her room. We pleaded with her, trying to work out what had happened. When she finally emerged, she was sobbing: 'Now you know everything about me.'

We hadn't even realised he had been talking about her. However, the conversation had triggered a relapse and Karen became paranoid. She accused my mother of poisoning her tea. We called in the Callan Park doctor. 'She has to be certified and readmitted. Once you sign her out, the police need to be involved,' he announced. The next morning our street was in uproar, with two ambulances and two police cars waiting while the orderlies put her in a straitjacket and carted her off to Callan Park.

After all the commotion had subsided, our friendly neighbour, Mrs Norrie, popped in. 'Where is Karen?' she asked. My mother said Karen was no longer with us.

'Is she back in Callan Park?' Mrs Norrie replied, matter-of-factly.

My mother was stunned. 'How did you know?' she gasped. This was absolutely confidential information. We hadn't told a soul.

'I used to work for a dentist as his receptionist in Dover Heights. He employed Karen but she went to Callan Park because she was pregnant. She lost her grip on reality and he couldn't keep her anymore.'

Everybody knew about her. It was an incredible coincidence. The child was adopted out, we discovered later. After Karen had returned to Callan Park, we also found some of her letters. One came from her mother. It turned out Karen was the daughter of a police officer in rural Germany. 'Who are these people that you're working for?' her mother wrote. 'The name Aram ... are they Jews?'

As my father was by then bedridden, we needed a replacement for Karen, and through the employment office found a Miss Molly Andrews, a typical country bumpkin. She came for the interview, accompanied by her cousin, a large overpowering woman. During the interview, Miss Molly sat with her head bowed in her lap and finally nodded that she would like to come and work for us. She started the next day and when evening fell my mother asked if she had her toothpaste and nightie for bed. Molly replied: 'My cousin said I should not bother as I would not last the day!' Molly stayed with us for 20 years, during which time my mother made a grande dame of her, with dresses and a silver fox cape given by her friends. She taught her how to cook and when they made a cake they found they were 20g short of what was needed. Asked how she would make up the shortfall, Molly thought for a while before replying: 'about two tablespoons!'

If I had any doubts whether A.R.A.M. Industries would survive, they were banished when David Jones asked me to manufacture lingerie, an endorsement that signalled my success to everyone. 'I haven't got the facilities,' I protested meekly. Nevertheless, they promised me an order and support, and I advertised for a designer. A Miss Quinn, who had a thriving bridal wear business in Market Street, came along and made the design. Unbeknown to me she was a very good friend of the head lingerie buyer at David Jones. When the buyer heard that Miss Quinn designed my range, she came around one day. 'If you make a nice range, we'll give you the Market Street window for your underwear,' she told my new designer.

One day my range appeared in the Market Street window of David Jones, which was the most coveted position for any manufacturer. Neither Osti nor Emstra had ever succeeded in achieving this recognition, but with my first range I had the premium position.

Frank Theeman and Emery Strassser were outraged. 'Why is David Jones doing this for him?' the grapevine reported. Eventually the truth leaked out. Pretty soon the inevitable happened: she received an offer from Theeman which, apart from a high salary, included shares in the Osti empire – an offer she couldn't refuse.

She followed the money, which was fine by me because I retained all her patterns. Overnight I became an underwear designer. On the one hand, I never again had the Market Street window, which wasn't so great for business. On the other hand, it meant Frank Theeman was not overly angry with me, which greatly enhanced my life expectancy.

That defection was just the start. Next, Emstra lured away my cutter, originally employed at the Emstra Junee factory. He came in one day and demanded a pay rise and I wanted to know why. He promptly walked out and left me with an uncut layer, which I stayed up all night to cut to meet an urgent order. I had learned how to cut at Silknit but I learned a new lesson in cloth cutting. I was using artificial silk (glovesilk), and you had to know how to use the cutter, because once you start and you do it the wrong way, the top layer of the silk can be easily dragged into the blade. As soon as I started, it got dragged. I spent all night cutting that layer with a pair of scissors by hand, so when the girls started in the morning they wouldn't know that I couldn't use the cutter. It was a terrible night. My hands were sore in the morning but the layer was cut and ready for sewing. As a result of this experience I became an expert cutter.

Out of necessity, I was transformed into a one-man show: cutting, designing and selling. I would leave home at five o'clock in the morning and would come home at night at eleven. I kept up this punishing schedule for about six months, until one night when I was doing the books a bolt of lightning struck the front of the factory. It blew me out of my chair and my mother insisted that I didn't come back late at night after that.

As well as manufacturing garments, I also imported novel accessories from Japan, and did very well with gimmicks. One of the most popular lines were the animals with moving eyes. They were plastic bubbles and had a little spot inside, and when they moved, the eyes moved with them. Kids loved it. Then I had Penny pants. I went to the bank, and bought bags full of pennies. My sewing girls took them home, polished them up and on every little panty we had a lace pocket, in which we put a shiny penny. Children and mothers both liked these. But they would take them back without a penny, to change for a different size. Eventually the retailers, including David Jones, wouldn't handle them because it was against their policy to give money away. But other stores loved it, particularly Myer in Melbourne. At Christmas time, I ran into trouble when Myer ordered 1000 dozen of these pants. The pennies weighed a ton in freight and the freight was far greater than the mark-up we made, so I had to give the idea away.

I also invented a packing machine for nylon and glove silk underwear. Initially, it was time-consuming to pack them in cellophane. I created a device with a pedal-operated plate that would move horizontally and push two prongs at the end to open a cellophane bag placed over the prongs. As the plate reversed, the garment was retained in the bag, ready for sealing. That appealed to retailers. I had a special flap made with the size and the colour, which went over the top. Although it was in cellophane, it looked like a box on the shelf. Alas, every good idea has a bad side effect. In this case, no customer would buy a garment unless they could inspect it, and they were all taken out of the cellophane bag. As a result, a lot of wrappers collected around the counter behind the girls, and the floor became very slippery. A few girls slipped on it, and I had to discontinue the wrappers due to safety concerns, which was a good thing in a way because I didn't have to spend the money on the cellophane. The big retailers liked my new ideas. I had an agent in Japan who made little kangaroos with moving eyes, complete with a pouch and joey. We put these things on the underwear and the pyjamas, and turnover jumped like the kangaroo ornaments.

Children's underwear and nightwear was quite profitable because there was less material than for grown-ups. That meant when nylon came in I could afford to make many more children's panties in different sizes, as against one slip for a woman, which took three times as much material, but with pretty similar labour costs.

Soon I was the biggest employer in the Auburn area and had made friends with the local solicitor, real estate agent, town clerk and council engineer. We became quite a happy little family, which helped me move into real estate on the side, while managing the lingerie business. Cumberland Associated Stores, my subsidiary company, so named because my original factory premises were in Cumberland Road, Auburn, started buying run-down properties in the locality, for eventual development into residential apartment blocks; they were in strong demand from the migrants settling there.

After repaying my loans, the surplus from my business went into mortgages with the local solicitor. I was now in a position to develop old houses that were put on the market after renovations. I built the units in apricot bricks to make them stand out against the traditional red brick ones. 'Why does everyone build in red textured brick? It looks so common,' I said to the real estate agent, and now friend, Des Eady.

'That's the only thing that'll sell,' he said.

'Let's try apricot-coloured bricks,' I replied. It was a great success.

The council was very much in favour of residential development, so we also built small units, blocks of six and blocks of twelve. In time, I developed a small shopping centre around the existing factory, through Cumberland Associated Stores.

A VERY BIG FAVOUR

While A.R.A.M. Industries prospered, my brother Arnold was also making his way in the world. After the war he became a draftsman engineer; one day he answered a newspaper advertisement from a company called Walter Heine and Partners, who were looking for an engineering graduate for their newly formed trading company. It was founded by Walter Heine and George Milton, who met when they were on the infamous SS *Dunera,* which brought 'enemy aliens' to Australia from London. These passengers later became known as the *Dunera* Boys, and were immortalised in a TV series of the same name. Walter Heine's parents had one of the largest textile mills in Germany, and he used his experience there to start an import/export company which became one of the largest privately owned in the world.

Arnold's first job was in sales promotions, helping Heine Brothers export everything from steel to dog droppings to India, and food to China. As the company grew, he rose through the ranks and they sent him around the world. When the company expanded into China, they asked Arnold to open an office for them. Before he left, he came to visit my parents and me in Sydney. My mother packed a knife, fork and spoon for the trip. When he arrived in China, we didn't hear from him for a while and my mother was quite certain that they'd found this knife in a suitcase and put him in jail. But after a few weeks a card arrived and my mother was relieved.

Right from the start, Arnold and I had totally different temperaments. He was more outgoing and enjoyed going to the greyhound races, while I sat at home and read books or studied. He was an outdoors man, I was an indoors man. My brother was also a company man, totally devoted to his boss. I was more the entrepreneurial type, prepared to run my own business. My background was more suitable for self-employment because of my accountancy background. Arnold gambled on greyhounds and horses but I was the greater risk-taker in life. In that sense, he took after my father, and I was very much like my mother, who was a worrier. She fretted about everything.

When we were growing up, Arnold wasn't what you would call a naturally dominant older brother. He was easy-go-lucky and he more or less left decisions about our parents to me. He went along with whatever I thought should be done for them, even while he was here. He was not as family-oriented as I was. My mother always promoted Arnold; when we arrived here he had to have a job before I did. From her perspective, my brother was the leading one. But Arnold left a lot of it to me. It was understood between us, and I accepted the responsibility as part of our family dynamic.

When Arnold first went to work for Heine Brothers in Melbourne, his flat on New South Head Road near Redleaf Pool was left vacant with a lease for another two years. My mother wanted a foreign student and approached the University of New South Wales. The only available person was a young Indian, Douglas Ram Samuj, who had been shunned by most landlords because of his very dark skin, and was desperate to find somewhere to live. On the day he was to view the apartment he stayed on the other side of the road, too scared to enter for fear of being rejected again. He loved the flat but said he only needed one bedroom as he would work in the kitchen – he was studying floral art and botany.

By day Douglas taught at a girls school and his pupils loved him. He told me I was welcome to use the flat as a city pad when I wanted a break from my parents at Strathfield. We became great friends, he was best man at my second wedding, and I guaranteed him for his Australian citizenship. Douglas eventually left Australia and settled in Rome, where he became a leading fabric designer and counted Jacqui Onassis and European royalty among his friends. The last time he visited was in the 1980s; he flew first class from Rome and arrived at my home in a chauffeur-driven limousine.

My brother would have been in his late twenties when he left Australia in the 1950s. From that point on, I was here alone with my parents. I always felt that I must take care of them. It didn't feel like an unfair burden, although sometimes I felt that Arnold could have taken a greater interest. I was the one who bought the first home for my parents. I lived with my parents until my thirties. He came back when he was passing through Sydney to go to Europe. But he was always a visitor; never here for any length of time.

Our mother took his absence well. As the first born, his career held a special place in her heart. If it meant that he had to travel, she supported that very much because he was so loyal to his company. Walter Heine also had his own shipping company, and my mother would have a special cabin on one of his ships to go to Japan. She visited quite often and developed a good relationship with his future wife, who dressed in a kimono and walked three steps behind my brother. My mother was very impressed with her.

He met his wife after being transferred from China to open the office in Japan. Then Heine Brothers opened an office in Manila in 1957, under the management of two men, Magtanggul Asa and Mr Riccaforte. When Mr Asa visited Australia to see the company's offices in Sydney and Melbourne, my brother asked me to show him around. Mr Asa had a vibrant personality and spoke freely about a wide range of subjects; everything from his opposition to our government's White Australia policy to book collecting, in particular his love of antique books.

During his visit Mr Asa spotted the antiquarian bookshop Berkelouw Books in King Street in the city, where he found some rare books on the history of the Philippines. He confided to me that due to government restrictions on bringing currency into the country, he regretted not having the money to buy them.

'How much would you need?' I asked.

'About one hundred pounds would do it,' he replied.

I liked Mr Asa and told him to meet me at my bank branch where I would give him the money. After I handed over the cash, he got out a notebook to write me a receipt. I tapped him on the shoulder.

'Mr Asa, if I did not trust you I would not lend you the money. As I do trust you, I don't need your receipt. You can pay the money back if I ever get to the Philippines.'

Mr Asa was dumbfounded and could not contain his gratitude. 'You are very generous man, Mr Aram. I will not forget your kindness and trust.'

I was taken aback by his reaction. After all, in the trading business, associates lent each other money all the time. In the end, I put it down to his exuberant, forceful nature and accepted his thanks with a polite nod. Before returning to Manila, he reminded me several times of his intention to pay me back.

Arnold had told me Asa was prominent in Filipino business circles but did not explain just how well connected he was. During the war, he told me freely, Asa collaborated with the Japanese and was a member of their interim government. After the war he was imprisoned but after being released from jail he quickly found his way back into business and government administration.

This may have explained why out of the blue, a year or so after meeting in Sydney, I received an invitation to the inauguration of Carlos Garcia and Diosdado Macapagal as President and Vice-President of the Philippines in December 1957. It was an appealing prospect. I was single at the time and I had no commitments to prevent me from going.

If I thought the invitation was exciting, I was completely unprepared for what happened on my arrival. When my flight touched down, a government limousine whisked me off to Manila's best hotel where Mr Asa and his charming wife were waiting for me. They organised a show of generosity normally reserved for foreign dignitaries. This included both formal and informal hospitality.

First, there was afternoon tea at the Royal Palace with the First Lady to be, her brother (the Minister for Aviation) and her two beautiful daughters. The afternoon tea at the palace afterwards was interrupted by an uninvited guest – a small field mouse which somehow evaded security and ran around the beautiful reception room. The First Lady and her two daughters leapt onto chairs while Mr Asa, the Aviation Minister and I tried to catch the mouse.

The informal hospitality was reserved for later in the week, when Mr Asa threw a private party at the hotel which included a sex romp with call girls. He arranged for all these women to come in to the hotel, which had a special room known as the 'sex room'; this was the in thing in Philippines entertainment at the time. It was my first and only experience of the sex romp. I remained an interested observer (although my wife does not believe this!).

Why was I feted like this? Apparently, Filipinos had a reputation for being untrustworthy and no one ever lent them money. When word got around that I had done so, without even wanting a receipt as proof of the loan, I became an instant celebrity. My gesture was unheard of in the country at the time. A local paper interviewed me: 'here was an Australian who had not only lent a Filipino £100 but he didn't even need a receipt,' it reported.

In a country like this, the inauguration ceremony was bound to have a few glitches. The presidential Lincoln taking Macapagal from the palace broke down a few hundred metres from the podium erected for the swearing-in ceremony. The assembled dignitaries, including me, were called upon to push it to the podium.

At the end of my visit, I politely refused Mr Asa's offer to repay the money (in pesos). We remained good friends until he died. Some years later, however, I gained an insight into the stereotype of Filipinos' alleged untrustworthiness regarding money. I arranged for a delegation headed by Mr Asa to attend an international business conference in Sydney sponsored by Sir Walter Scott's advisory organisation, and guaranteed their stay at what was then the Hotel Australia. True to form, Mr Asa's account was paid properly.

Some years later, after Mr Asa's death, Mr Riccaforte took over from him. We got to know each other well but I didn't develop the same level of friendship with him. Following Asa's death, Riccaforte headed another delegation to Australia and asked me to make similar arrangements at the same hotel. Since I didn't know him as well, I asked the hotel to make their own arrangements for payment from Riccaforte's party. A few months after they had returned home, the hotel rang me to say the account was overdue. I assumed it was an oversight and the account was eventually paid.

In between pushing presidential limousines in Manila, I was fending off business suitors in Sydney until I received an offer too good to refuse.

In 1958 my first employer in the clothing business, Silknit, offered to buy my whole business, giving me 20,000 shares and appointing me manager. However, after starting my new position it became clear that in the thirteen years since Morris Epstein had taken me under his wing, Silknit had not kept pace with the times, using equipment that was slow and out of date. I tried to shift production to Fiji to ease labour costs, which threatened profitability right across the industry. A lot of firms were going offshore at that time.

In 1960 I was appointed managing director and moved into the office where Mr Epstein first interviewed me, the one with the panelled walls. But although the company had appointed an astute board, including Sir Bertram Stevens (the former Premier of NSW), the Japanese left Silknit for dead. They copied the designs and manufactured them far more cheaply. I could see that the business would either be sold or taken over, so in 1962 I applied to study at Harvard University and presented references from Sir Bertram Stevens and my first mentor, Major Murray Jones, from de Havilland. I retained a close relationship with Major Murray Jones over the years and I was touched by his enthusiastic support in this reference, which encapsulated my whole life in Australia:

> I have known Mr Henri Walter Aram for some 24 years, ever since he joined the de Havilland organisation in Sydney as a junior clerk.
>
> He came to us under the grave disadvantage of being a newcomer to our country, who had been educated in his earliest years in a foreign land. At the time I was General Manager of de Havilland Aircraft Pty Ltd, and I was very interested in watching his progress in overcoming these difficulties, the measure of which is demonstrated by the academic qualifications he now possesses.
>
> He served with our company right through the 1939–45 War, and we found him to be capable, conscientious and hardworking, so

that, when he felt compelled to move to wider fields, we were very sorry to lose his services. However, he has been very successful in the work he has undertaken, and as I have kept in touch with him right up to the present time, I am sure his decision to leave us was correct.

I know him to be most honest in his outlook, very competent at anything he undertakes, and that he still retains that youthful ambition for yet greater successes.

I understand that Mr Aram desires to attend the Advanced Management Programme at Harvard University and I have no hesitation in stating that should he attend such a course, he will do well possessing, as he does to a very high degree, the intelligence, and adaptability, as well as the capacity for leadership that it [*sic*] will enable him to develop still further.

13th November, 1961

Because the company was in the process of being wound down, the Silknit board refused to give an undertaking to Harvard that, once I had completed the degree, I would return to them. So my application came to nought. A few months later, Silknit was sold to the O'Connell Corporation.

A.R.A.M. Industries factory at Auburn (before and after)

Manila, 1957: the Christmas Party at the Riccafortes'

Dancing with Mrs Asa at the same party

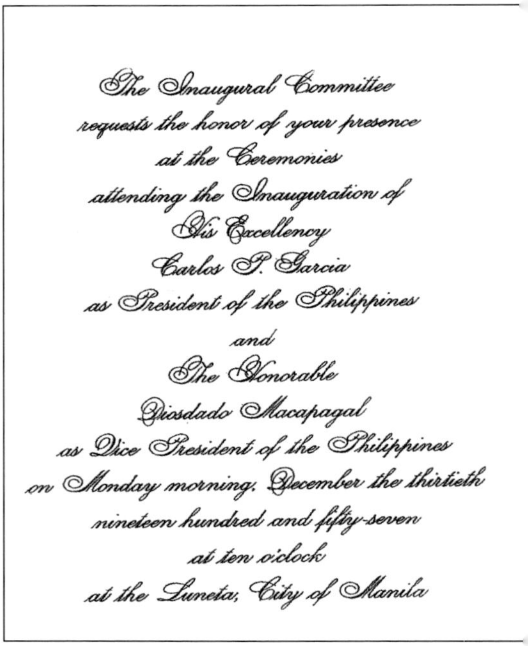

The Inaugural Committee
requests the honor of your presence
at the Ceremonies
attending the Inauguration of
His Excellency
Carlos P. Garcia
as President of the Philippines
and
The Honorable
Diosdado Macapagal
as Vice President of the Philippines
on Monday morning, December the thirtieth
nineteen hundred and fifty-seven
at ten o'clock
at the Luneta, City of Manila

Invitation to the inauguration of the new Filipino president

FREUDIAN SLIP

My second period at Silknit was intertwined with a series of difficult moments in my personal life. The year after I was appointed manager of the company, my father died at the age of 82. During his last years, he was bedridden in our Strathfield home. I remember distinctly that I took the day off when he died. I sat by his bedside and saw him breathe his last breath. My own heart missed a beat. It was the first – and last – time my heart missed a beat. It was an experience I'd never had before and never wanted to have again. His passing was not just a loss for my mother and me (Arnold had moved overseas by then) but was keenly felt by our family dachshund, which was very attached to him. While he was bedridden, he would rattle a railing on his bed at night if he wanted something. After my father died, that same rattle occurred. I had the next room to him, and I went out to see what caused the noise. It was as if the ghost of my father had returned. The dachshund was so nervous, and pined after him. There was a sliding door and the dog stuck his nose in the door and tried to get through to be with him. These moments stay in your mind forever.

The years of pressure and uncertainty leading up to the takeover exacted a heavy toll on my own health. I developed a gall bladder problem; it ran in the family; both my parents had gall bladder issues.

The doctor recommended an operation and my mother was against surgery. But while she was on holiday in Japan visiting my brother, I had an attack during my last days at Silknit and was forced to have emergency surgery to have my gall bladder removed. When I returned from hospital, my secretary arranged for me to go to the Gold Coast to rest.

She booked me into the Broadbeach Hotel, part of a hotel group managed by Oliver Shaul (later a restaurateur and owner of The Summit restaurant at the top of Australia Square in Sydney), who had been a friend of mine since our early teens. We had shared the same fate, moved in the same circles and had identical backgrounds. Unbeknown to me, Oliver arranged a party for me at Broadbeach and intended to introduce me to a young German widow he knew from Melbourne who had also just arrived. As fate would have it, I could not make the party and my intended match came to the attention of a grazier from Griffith in regional New South Wales. 'You have missed the boat,' Olli (as I called him) lamented.

One day, sitting at the pool, I spied an attractive young woman who stood out from the others. I noticed that she was reading the autobiography of Sigmund Freud. A Polish man sitting near me noticed my interest and whispered: 'She is German.'

'So what?' I said.

'They're all Nazis,' he replied.

I turned and walked away but shot a parting glance at the woman in question. (Little did I know at the time that this was the 'young lady' Olli wanted to introduce me to at his party. He only told my current wife, Robin, years later.)

Next day, I went down to the pool again. The Polish man didn't show his face this time but the woman was there. I sat down beside her at the pool. I was confident making ladies' underwear but uncomfortable about talking to them in swimming costumes. I remembered the book.

'You're reading Sigmund Freud,' I said.

'Yes,' she replied quietly, slightly quizzically.

'You know that he is a Jew?' I continued.

Her mouth tightened. 'What have you got against the Jews?' she shot back sharply.

It was my first contact with her and I knew it wasn't a conventional approach to talking up a woman. But I wanted to test her, see what her reaction would be. My instinct was right. As we talked, she turned out to be very pro-Jewish, and was initially prickly about my line of conversation. Slowly, however, we moved on to more comfortable subjects.

This young woman, in her twenties, was a widow. She had been staying at the hotel for a week and spent most of the time fending off the unwanted attentions of a rich grazier. (Do graziers always go for European women, I wondered, reflecting on Charlotte.)

This woman's name was Christina Haarburger (maiden name Nieke). She was German but not Jewish, and she had been married to a Jewish Holocaust survivor in Melbourne, a German leather worker who migrated to Australia after the war. He lived underground in Holland during the war, hiding between the floorboards, just like Anne Frank, and because he was deprived of sunlight, had a lung problem ever after.

Christina's sister Irina worked for this man in his Melbourne leather factory, and she brought her out here as an assisted migrant to work in the factory with them. Christina was very gifted with her hands. She could knit, make belts, hats, virtually any type of clothing or accessory. Eventually she ran his business, and he married her. However, his lung condition worsened and soon he became terminally ill. Christina became pregnant in his last years and because of his health she decided to have an abortion. Before he died, her husband told her: 'Try and marry another Jew, because they make good husbands.' All up, they had five years of marriage, full of ill-health and medical problems.

Her husband's words must have echoed in Christina's ears from beyond the grave. After he died, her sister Irma told her to go for a holiday to rest, rejuvenate, get her strength back. That's when I met her at the Gold Coast. But there were other hurdles first. The grazier from Griffith wanted Christina to meet his mother but he warned her that his mother didn't like foreigners. 'Thank you very much, I'm not interested,' Christina told him. She once had a boyfriend back in Germany whose mother also felt she wasn't good enough for her son. That's why she had left Germany in the first place.

The grazier took the hint and left; then it was time for Christina to leave too. As she drove up in the car, I could see her from my balcony. I waved to her and she waved back. On the strength of that exchange, she decided to extend her stay for another week. I was hooked from the start and by the end of that week I wanted her to come and live with me. 'Come to Sydney,' I urged her. But Christina had a button shop in St Kilda, the seaside Melbourne suburb with a large Jewish and European population. It was the only button shop in Melbourne. Although the business traded well, her husband's illness left her heavily in debt. The bank wanted to close her down. I went to Melbourne, vowed to fix it, whatever the problem, and spoke to the bank manager. It was more complicated than I had anticipated.

My mother saw the telephone bills between Melbourne and Sydney. 'I think it would be cheaper if you married the girl,' she said. I introduced them, calling her Tina to family and friends to soften the Christian aspect of her name. My mother took to her immediately; everyone loved her. I had old relatives and she looked after them. She had a wonderful heart. 'You can't blame all the Germans,' I found myself saying. I had a school friend in Israel whose parents were murdered at Auschwitz, and when I told him about Tina he was disgusted.

'How can you marry a German?' he sputtered.

'I take people for what they are – I don't blame the new generation for what their parents did,' I replied calmly. When my friend later came out to Australia and met Tina, he changed his tune and they soon became very good friends.

Tina was eleven years younger than me. The age difference did not present a problem. But my indecision did. We were in love, but like many men I couldn't commit; I had trouble making up my mind. She declared that she was planning to return to Germany, as there was nothing to make her stay in Australia. She had everything ready, tickets and dates booked.

Finally, at the end of yet another long phone call from Sydney to Melbourne, I made my intentions clear. 'I think we should legitimise this,' I said down the line.

'What, are you going to adopt me?' she chuckled. Tina had a great sense of humour. When the laughter died down, she said yes. I was 500 miles away, invisible and I wasn't down on one knee, but she knew it was a marriage proposal.

We married in 1962, a year or so after meeting at that hotel, at the registry office opposite St Mary's Cathedral at Hyde Park in Sydney. A reception was held at the Hotel Australia, attended by a lot of friends I had made from Rotary, which I joined when I worked at Silknit. My best man was Douglas Ram Samuj, the Indian student who I befriended when he rented out Arnold's apartment in Double Bay. None of Tina's family was there. She had fallen out with her sister, Irma, the one who sponsored her to come to Melbourne. They were very different personalities: Tina was attractive and refined, Irma was relatively unsophisticated. Nevertheless, she also had romantic designs on the Dutch man who employed her, but when he took a shine to Tina instead, Irma's jealousy poisoned the relationship between them.

After the wedding we moved into the T & G Building, a fashionable Art Deco apartment block on the corner of Park and Elizabeth streets in the city centre. I had been taken by its style ever since I caught the bus into the city to work at David Jones when we first arrived in Sydney. My bus stop was right outside the T & G and every day I peered inside at the spacious foyer, where a liveried concierge stood in charge. One day I went in to have a look around and put my name on the list of interested tenants, should an apartment ever become available. I had been on the list for twenty years. Our many interesting neighbours in the T & G included a Mrs Shartel, whose late husband was the founder of the Email whitegoods company. This woman took a fancy to Tina and introduced her to Nola Dekyvere, who was to become the doyenne of Sydney socialites in the 1950s and 1960s at the Black and White Committee. Under Mrs Dekyvere's patronage, Tina was elected vice-president.

TAKING STOCK OF RUPERT

Life with Tina was wonderful but I still had to work. The year that we married, Silknit was taken over, I couldn't go to Harvard, I didn't have a job. My career was at a crossroads. However, as my personal life flowered, a new road also opened in my working life, through a good friend in Melbourne who happened to be a client of the leading stockbroking firm, Cutten and Harvey. The firm approached me to ask if I was interested in moving into stockbroking. I had earlier met the firm when Silknit bought me out and offered me shares in the company. They were my first share market holding and I got to know stockbrokers who were interested in acquiring or selling my shares.

Cutten and Harvey had just floated the oil exploration company Santos and wanted to open a Sydney office to raise capital for a new float of News Limited, which was owned and run by Rupert Murdoch. They had close connections to News through Rupert's father, Sir Keith Murdoch. 'Why don't you run our Sydney office?' they asked. Cuttens wanted a city office. I had been living in an apartment in the T & G Building, which was close to the stock exchange building. It was ideal for the stockbrokers' needs.

Coincidentally, it also led to my discovering and collecting Satsuma pottery and vases, which are the Japanese equivalent of French Sevres porcelain. At the back of the T & G Building was Lawsons auctioneering house, a famous institution in Sydney art and collecting circles, which I frequented in my spare time. One day, the head auctioneer, Max Lawson, had two big vases that he described as 'exquisite'. I bid $800 for one and $1000 for the other, and the *Australian Financial Review* carried a story that 'some mad investment adviser' had bought these two vases. I was hooked. From that point on, whenever Lawson had rare Satsumas, they would ring me.

Initially, I flew to Adelaide for training every week and came back to Sydney at weekends. I operated from the T & G Building for a while and then opened an office in Bond Street, closer to the stock exchange. The firm was happy and offered me 80,000 News Limited shares to place for Sydney clients. I found one, a prominent businessman named Sir Robert Crighton-Brown, chairman of the company Edward Lumley, who said he would be interested, but wanted two million shares. This was too many, and risked diluting the company ownership. I consulted the principals of the firm and after some negotiation Rupert Murdoch agreed to sell him one million shares, on the understanding that he wasn't connected to Lord Thompson, the Fleet Street media mogul in London. That transaction set up the office for the next two years.

I didn't actually get to meet Rupert Murdoch but I went close. Murdoch invited all the staff from Cutten and Harvey to dinner one night at his home in Darling Point. At the last minute Rupert didn't turn up because suddenly he had to have an operation for haemorrhoids. Amazingly, the next morning he went on a cruise on his yacht, within a day of the operation. His wife attended the dinner but Rupert was indisposed. I didn't deal directly with Rupert. That was done for the firm by Hubert Harvey, one of the principals.

I learned a lot about investing during those years but my best investment during that period, in fact for all my life, was not in shares or property. It was a Dale Carnegie course, which taught me public speaking. I was reserved by nature, my parents had not encouraged us to speak up as children back in Berlin – that was not the German way. I lacked confidence and my sales pitch was stiff, formal. This would have been bad enough for other products, but when you're a grown man selling children's underwear, mainly to women, it put me at a distinct disadvantage.

Ever since childhood I had found it difficult to speak in front of others, and of course in public. Selling clothes had reminded me of this handicap so in 1964 I answered an ad for a Dale Carnegie course. The tutor at this course was a dynamic man called George Renwick, an insurance salesman who taught the course on the side. After the first few sessions, George took me aside and gave me a gentle admonishment: 'We do not often get people of your calibre, Henri. While you know what you're talking about, you present it in a way that is above people's heads. Talk to their interests and level of understanding and you will impress and win their support! Talk in their interests, Henri, not in yours. Talk about something they understand – like gardening.'

'But I know nothing about gardening,' I protested.

'That's why it is the very subject you should be discussing with them.'

So I took his advice and on presentation night, while everyone else spoke about their home, their work, etc. – I pulled a pair of nylon undies out of my pocket, and said to the group:

'Why is this like a barbed wire fence?

'It protects the property but doesn't restrict the vision.'

This brought the house down and I was elected president of the group for the next year. That course helped me all my life.

Years later, a man named Stuart Renwick made an appointment to see me. I took one look at him: 'You wouldn't be the son of George?'

'Yes, I am. And I know all about you because my father never stopped talking about you.' Stuart Renwick became a surgeon and later, a client of mine.

BACK TO BERLIN

I introduced a new client to Cutten and Harvey named Edward Hershon, who had started the bra company, Hestia (Holds Every Sized Tit In Australia). My mother knew Hershon before he started Hestia; she had helped him with bra designs. When Silknit was broken up, Hershon bought A.R.A.M. Industries and approached me to see if I could join Hestia. In 1965 I accepted his offer and joined as assistant general manager, but it was not a very happy relationship. I was caught between an ageing father and playboy son, a dilemma that reminded me of my troubles at Emstra, and I left a year later. I needed a break and went with Tina on a six-month overseas trip across Asia and Europe, promoting Australian investments. I also visited stock exchanges in London, Berlin and other major cities. We finished up with a holiday in sunny Spain.

Of course, Germany was much more than a visit to the stock exchange. Tina's mother was still living there and we visited her on a delayed honeymoon, in 1966. I had mixed feelings about going back. I have always felt you cannot blame the present generation for the misdeeds of their parents or grandparents, which in a way helped me. But I was very disillusioned about what was being taught about the Holocaust and the war. Nowadays, people speak more freely but they also say, ‘it’s history, it’s in the past’. They don’t want to confront the past, and how it echoes into the present.

Visiting my old family home and neighbourhood in Berlin was easier than visiting the new in-laws. Here were two families thrown together by marriage but with totally different backgrounds. The husband’s side came from peasant stock and built a prosperous building supply business in Schwabach near Nuremberg, courtesy of the Nazi Party, of which they were members. Hitler held his rallies there before the war. Tina’s immediate family were East Germans called ‘Ossies’(they were regarded as second-grade citizens) at the time. Because they refused to join the party they were denied lucrative business contracts and could no longer obtain the licences needed to operate the kiosk-style dining rooms which were a feature of most town halls in major German cities.

They were impoverished by the regime while party members, like the building suppliers, flourished. Their Nazi membership was revealed while I searched for something in the attic: I discovered a large picture of Hitler surrounded by former German emperors at their time of glory. This would only be found in the homes of true believers in their Fuehrer, and not normally in a household that didn’t support him.

I did not feel comfortable at certain comments, particularly when her brother-in-law said to me, over a Christmas dinner: ‘Not everything that Hitler did was wrong, of course, but the Jewish Problem should have been handled differently.’

I will never forget that comment.

‘Tell me, what was the Jewish Problem?’ I asked him.

‘Quite frankly, I don’t know,’ he replied. Before anyone could say anything, his mother suddenly interjected: ‘Henri is the best decorator of Christmas trees …’

Another time a family member suggested that the Jews shouldn’t complain because they queued up for the death chambers. ‘You can see it in the photos, they could have revolted,’ she continued.

'Come off it. Revolt?' I said, barely able to restrain myself.

I later came to see that they weren't educated. This side of the family, like so many others, had never been told what really happened. It took an unwitting remark over a family dinner to make me see the invisible layer of silence. I don't think the Germans had really learned. Not at that time, anyway. A lot of people would talk about the positive things that Hitler did. By that they meant he put the masses of unemployed people back to work, building the autobahns with the money they confiscated from the Jews. Although I believe you cannot blame young people for what their parents did and said, I would say the world, and the Germans in particular, have really learned nothing.

Tina was clearly uncomfortable with these members of her extended family. She had arguments with one of her sisters over the war. A second sister, Irina, the one who migrated to Australia and sponsored Tina after her, had been in a refugee camp before coming here. She married an unemployed man, which created friction. Her family suffered under the regime while the other side thrived. That makes it very difficult when you're talking about Germans, especially with those from the West and the East – two opposing factions.

On the advice of my mother-in-law, we headed to Czechoslovakia and the beautiful old spa town of Karlovy Vary, which she recommended as a cure for my ongoing gall bladder problem. The country was still under Soviet domination, it was still two years before the Prague Spring uprising of 1968, and Karlovy Vary was a major holiday spot. Local doctors would assign visitors to certain springs, each containing different combinations of minerals deemed suitable for specific complaints. You put a small bottle under a tap and drank the very hot water that dribbles out. Every morning you could see people sipping from small spouted bottles as they walked around the magnificent countryside surrounding the historic town centre.

It was on one of these walks that a man emerged from behind a bush and exclaimed: 'I Love You'. I didn't blink and kept walking, all the way back to my hotel, hoping that he didn't follow me. The next morning Tina accompanied me on another walk and the same thing happened. This time he was accompanied by another man, who engaged me in English and apologised for his friend's outburst. He is Russian and speaks no other language, was the explanation.

He knew only two phrases in English: 'I Love You' and 'Nyet I Love You' (the opposite).

As a journalist later explained it, when I described our experience to him, in an article in the *Australian* (July 1966):

His conversation would go something like this …

'I love you cognac.'

'Nyet I love you cigarettes' – the addition of the Nyet being all he imagined necessary to indicate his dislike.

The remainder of his communication, which Tina assures me worked extremely well, was conducted by means of drawings and pantomime dances.

This man was trying to say he wanted to meet with Tina and me. Like most men who laid eyes on Tina, couldn't take his eyes off her. His name was Nikolai Nikogosyan and he was one of Russia's most famous sculptors. He presented us with a signed book containing pictures of busts he had made of Stalin, Roosevelt and other world renowned figures. And now he wanted to make a bust of Tina. We liked the idea, even though we knew little about him. However, the logistics were delicate, as he was being watched by the KGB and the process had to be an undercover operation. After careful negotiations, we agreed that they would pick up Tina in a car late at night, drive to the friend's study, and after a two-hour sitting return her to our hotel under identical security cover. There were about eight sittings and although the artist wasn't entirely happy with his finished work we had to leave for home – taking the fragile plaster cast with us.

Our next challenge came at the border, where we had to convince suspicious guards that the mysterious plaster bust did not contain contraband or foreign currency. Eventually we got it back to Australia and had the plaster cast in bronze. (It turned out to be Nikogosyan's only work in the West until my brother Arnold, on a visit to his studio in Moscow, had his own portrait sculptured; a work that went back to his home in Tokyo.)

Had the border guards known about Tina's early years after the war, they might have not let her through. Here is how that article in the *Australian* described it:

> As an adventurous (foolhardy?) 17-year-old, Tina survived the bitter, grim days in post-war Berlin by ferrying pieces of porcelain from East to West. 'It was dangerous,' she admits. 'But in those days we would do anything to survive. There was no food in East Berlin and I couldn't stay there anyway.
>
> 'I'd been working with an anti-communist group, distributing leaflets and such, and when one of my girlfriends was arrested, I knew I had to head for the West.'
>
> But at first the West didn't want her and without proper papers she could not get work. So she made a precarious living transporting precious items of porcelain (mainly old Dresden and Meissen) to the West where eager Americans were waiting to buy.

This fragile livelihood almost ended in disaster when, dressed in a headdress to make her look like an impoverished peasant, she tried to shift an eagerly awaited piece known as Napoleon's Flight across the border in a pram. The guards got wise and she escaped only by abandoning the pram, and the art work, and jumping on a departing suburban train to West Berlin.

Years later, I transferred the bust to the care of Tina's niece, Karin, in Germany, to ensure it would stay in her family and be appreciated. During the preparation of this book, I emailed her to inquire about some details. In turn she contacted Nikogosyan's son, who lives in Ireland. When he heard from my niece, he went to Germany and stayed with her for a few days. During that time he revealed that his father, who was born in 1918, is alive and well and living in Moscow, aged 93, and in fact keen to re-establish contact with me. He emailed me last year with his details.

Tina at home in Edgecliff during the 1960s

The bust of Tina by the Armenian artist Nikogosyan

Nikogosyan in his studio with Arnold during a visit

I present this book to Christine ~~and~~ Henry ~~Nancy (could be Hanzay)~~ Aramian to prove my love for them as the first people I came to ~~[struck out]~~ know in Australia and whom I came to love.

I beg ~~from~~ God to give them long life and happiness.

~~[struck out]~~

Nigoghos Nigoghosian
9th June 1968

Gai (Signature) Vai (signature)

An inscription in his book to us. The artist's subjects included Roosevelt, Stalin and Churchill.

I met Tina at the Broadbeach Hotel on the Gold Coast early in 1962. We were married a year later in Sydney.

My brother Arnold with his wife Yuki and their two sons, Anthony (left) and Alexander (right)

My mother with her two daughters-in-law, Yuki and Tina, Arnold and my best man, Douglas Ram Samuj, in 1972

(Above) Outside Woollahra Council in 1983
(Left) The poster for my 1980 campaign to be re-elected onto Woollahra Council. I was an alderman from 1977 until 1987.

HOT TIPS AND FREE ADVICE

On my return from Europe, I faced a choice: continue my career in finance or return to clothing. I had some investments and property to manage but had no specific job, so in 1967 I enrolled in a two-week program at the University of Armidale in northern NSW, an intensive training course for senior executives. It proved to be a profitable decision; among the attendees were two senior partners from the large stockbroking firm, Ord Minett. We became friendly and they invited me to join their firm, which I did, just in time for the mining boom of the 1970s – the boom where Poseidon reached $300 a share, and Tasminex jumped $100 in a day.

The partners in the firm were Jack Minnett, Charlie Ord, Brian Wiesener and others. They demanded a high level of ethical standards from advisers, which suited my sensibility. Clients' interests always came first, no matter what. One day a man rang up, wanting a broker. He wanted to buy $500,000 of a speculative mining stock. 'I can't handle that,' I told him. 'I'll put you on to a senior partner.' The senior partner said they would buy them, provided he brought in the cash on the same day. A few hours later he turned up with two bodyguards, a gun and a suitcase full of money.

He tipped out the suitcase full of money and said: 'Count it.' There were no questions asked.

They were exciting days. I had two phones going all the time. Bill Singleton, a Western Australian businessman and director of the mining company Tasminex, stumbled off a plane and started talking up his company to the assembled media. 'We have struck massive sulphides in our drilling, larger than Poseidon' (which sent the share price into orbit from $1 to $18 in a single day). 'It's a bigger mine than Poseidon,' he shouted, drunkenly, and continued in this vein for days to anyone who would listen. I thought I was going to make my fortune with Tasminex, but it didn't turn out that way. In 1972 the boom turned to bust and I sensed it was time for me to move on. Ord Minett reduced their staff and we parted ways amicably.

There were also major changes on the domestic front. That same year Tina and I adopted a daughter and moved into a comfortable house, Knowle, on New South Head Road in Double Bay. Tina's abortion to her first husband did not go smoothly and a few years into our marriage we learned that she had been left with a blocked fallopian tube, which meant she couldn't have children. After several years of applications and meetings, finally we were granted permission to adopt a young girl we called Jackie.

By this time, through her introduction to Nola Dekyvere, Tina had become active with the Black and White Committee, Sydney's leading social and charity organisation. She had a way with people that put them at ease, and I enjoyed the social openings she created. Tina was also a gifted fashion designer, and combined with her social activities, she was frequently photographed in the fashion pages of the newspapers and magazines. She made her own hats, belts, dresses – and over the years she won three Black and White Committee Best

Dressed awards. It cost her $50 or $100, and other people would pay $5000 and $10,000 for a dress. And yet, she won.

We had a wide social circle, including the former Prime Minister, Sir William McMahon, and his wife Sonia. Our daughters were in the same class at Ascham. We used to meet at school, at the parents' meetings. I also crossed paths again with Frank Theeman, who by then had moved into property development. One night he invited us to a fundraising night at his fancy house in Tivoli Avenue, Rose Bay. Theeman was running around in a state of high energy, excited at social whirl around him. Sir Percy Spender, the diplomat, who we saw often at these functions, turned to Tina, sitting next to him: 'Who is that funny little man?' he quipped. 'Sir Percy, he is your host.'

The Fairfax family, then owners of the Fairfax newspaper and publishing empire, also became part of our social circle. In particular, Lady Mary would invite us over for dinner at Fairwater. In truth I think it was more because of Tina. Those were the days. I'll never forget their security arrangement at Fairwater – a barking dog. When nobody was at home, they had a record behind the main door that played the sounds of a party as though there were hundreds of people talking, or a dog barking. It was a brilliant idea for a security arrangement.

In the real world outside of Sydney's Eastern Suburbs old-money crowd, life was harder, especially for all the people who lost their hard-earned money after the market crash. While working at Ord Minnett, I met John Valder, who was the Chairman of the Sydney Stock Exchange. There had been so much speculation and lying during the boom that one day at a corporate function I took Valder aside and suggested he start up an advisory service at the Exchange. 'Why don't you teach people the basics?' I said. I was always a fundamentals investor but I saw how people got carried away by the lure of fast money. 'People have lost money, but they don't need to lose money if they at least know the basics,' I explained.

Valder liked the idea straight away but turned instead to a man called Bruce Bond, who was already employed by the Exchange as its educational officer. I was upset, to say the least, to see my idea given to someone else. Bond had a brusque, direct manner and many people felt uncomfortable; the project did not take off. My disappointment soon turned to satisfaction, however, when Valder came back to me six months later and asked me if I would give it ago.

So after four years at Ord Minnett I was offered an office space at street level of the Sydney Stock Exchange building in O'Connell Street, hung up the 'Stock Exchange Advisory' shingle, and opened for business in May 1974. It offered me the opportunity to educate the wider public about the workings of the stock market and how each individual could take advantage of the capitalist system and apply it to serve their best personal interests.

It was great step in the right direction and the retainer offered to me by the Exchange provided income security. Bruce Bond and I were to work side by side, which turned out to be wishful thinking. On hearing the news, Bond became jealous and our relationship continued, strained. Somehow, however, we managed. The Exchange advertised the service extensively in the media, hosting free lunchtime seminars, and the public took to the service in droves. In time stock exchanges worldwide introduced their own versions of the service. Locally, the response became overwhelming. 'So great was the public response to newspaper advertisements, that these had to be discontinued,' the *Australian Women's Weekly* wrote in an interview with me soon after the service began in 1974. It promoted itself largely by word of mouth and media interviews.

I likened myself to a doctor. 'I am the GP who directs patients to the specialists from whom they can get the help they need,' I told the *Women's Weekly*. 'It's no use sending a conservative old lady to a young chap with long hair. They must be compatible. Confidence is the basis of the relationship.'

Soon I had 30 to 40 people coming in a week, from all backgrounds, but mainly ordinary investors who didn't know how to deal with brokers and felt shy about calling them 'cold'. I assessed the client, their temperament and the risk profile, and then I matched them with the right broker. There were all types. One day a man came in with an old suitcase. He sat down and opened it in front of me. There was $100,000 in notes inside, clearly the result of a robbery. He wanted me to recommend a broker. Instead, I notified the police, who came and arrested him.

In addition to providing one-on-one advice, I also conducted radio and television interviews, often with a live audience, and held lunchtime seminars in the ASX auditorium with a range of speakers. Investment advisers discussed what constituted an investment-grade stock, mining hopefuls or established producers talked about how to strike it rich, bond and fixed-interest securities experts shed light on how their products and markets worked. These talks filled the auditorium to capacity and heightened the profile of my service.

The media soon recognised its impact. 'The Oracle of O'Connell Street,' the *Sun* newspaper declared in November 1974.

> Millions of dollars have sought Henri Aram's advice since he put up his shingle as the Sydney Stock Exchange investment adviser six months ago. Ironically, very little of the money has gone into the market. Aram believes most has been invested in short-term, fixed-interest stock.
>
> The big surprise for Aram has been the amount of money his inquirers have to invest – $400,000 in one instance. After expecting people with small nest eggs, he has found a big

number have five-figure amounts, mainly from superannuation.
Aram has kept a tally of inquiries and it comes to more than $4 million. He is adamant about the impartiality of his advice. 'People must be able to talk to me frankly, without feeling obligated.'

The *Women's Weekly* interview chronicled the amazing range of people who rang me for advice.

> One lady of 80 rang him from a retirement village wanting to invest $12,000 for 'her old age'. Since she was unable to visit the city she did not know how to best achieve her objective.
>
> Mr Aram arranged for a stockbroker to visit her in the village, and in the process he was able to help three of her friends there as well.
>
> Another little old lady confided to Mr Aram that she could talk more freely to him than to her son because 'she did not know me, and she did not want her son to know how much money she had saved for fear he might stop her weekly allowance'.
>
> 'We had an old man, 80-odd, with hundreds of thousand of dollars in cash to invest. He was someone who should have sought advice on estate planning years before.' (He lived with a much younger woman and was worried that she would find out he had a few million in the bank!)
>
> Whether people save or not depends on their early background and the example set by parents, according to Mr Aram. 'There are those who look on savings as a financial discipline. Others believe that the government should look after them in their old age.'

Within a year, I was doing nearly 100 interviews a week, the *Australian* newspaper reported in May 1975. 'Mr Peter Marshman, general manager of the Sydney Exchange, said that the service had assisted people from all walks of life with greatly differing amounts of money to invest,' the article continued.

Not everyone was happy. A number of brokers were jealous, thinking I favoured some over others. ('He gets some comebacks after brokers have compared notes over lunch,' the *Sun* reported.) It wasn't straightforward. Every broker was different – some were speculative, some only wanted the big clients. Broking in those days was different. People weren't afraid to give advice. There was Ord Minett, there was ABS White, Hordern, Utz and Bode, and a host of others. They were people you could trust, the same as a bank manager. That's non-existent now. In those days, business was done with a handshake. I would interview people, give them my spiel that I had nothing to sell but commonsense. Even before the Australian Securities and Investments Commission (ASIC) made it mandatory, I told them they had to tell me about their backgrounds. It was my modus operandi. I would find out their risk profile, how they were placed, where their money was coming from, what the income was. I made it quite clear that I wasn't trying to stickybeak into their affairs but that I must know this information to give any worthwhile advice. My advice has always been based on the capacity and the risk profile of people, and to make people understand that the stock market was not a bond issue, with a guaranteed rate of return. I tried to convince them that, especially in times of crisis, the return *of* money became more important than the return *on* money.

I have always made it clear to people I wasn't into quick money. Speculators used to pump me for tips but I'm not a tipster. People came to realise it wasn't my business to make a quick buck. Some of them gave me information that wasn't really true because they wanted to speculate. They took my ideas, then went to other advisers who implemented them. Some lost a lot of money. I never took these people as clients.

Before the mining boom of 1972, trading was an honest business. You could go to your stockbroker for honest advice like your bank manager. But electronic trading has totally hit that on the head. It ushered in a new era of greed. Today, nobody is prepared to give financial advice because compliance regulations make it a wealth hazard. People don't have to be responsible for their actions anymore. They think they can go to the Financial Ombudsman and get their money back if a stock loses value. People don't have to accept responsibility. In my day when I was a stockbroker, it was a matter of trust. You trusted the client and the client trusted you. You didn't take advantage of them and they would understand market volatility.

The reputation of my advisory service spread quickly. Melbourne started its own version a little over a year after mine (in September 1975), then bourses overseas created them as a public service. This publicity turned me into something of a media celebrity, which gave me the confidence to start my own investment advisory service in 1978.

I used my best asset – my name – as a selling point, calling the company ARAM (Allied Research and Media Services, later changed to A.R.A.M. Investment Services). I had clients large and small. The big ones included the Bank of Adelaide, because I had managed Cutten and Harvey's Sydney office, and we dealt with the Bank of Adelaide. As it turned out, the Bank of Adelaide was in my current building, 275 George Street, at Wynyard, and they gave me premises on the second floor. It was a risk. Although I had half the floor, there was no street presence or visibility.

In private business, I continued to apply the same philosophy that I used at the Exchange Service: independent advice tailored to individual needs. Many of the small clients became good friends: from modest beginnings in the 1970s they became millionaires 30 years later. Among them was a pensioner couple with $50,000 on deposit with the Commonwealth Bank who I persuaded instead to buy the bank's shares at $5 each, with the undertaking that I would buy them back at that price if the shares failed to perform. The only problem they encountered was the loss of their pension as the shares climbed to over $50 each.

The office location worked out much better than expected. I have been in this same building for 40 years, with one gap, when I moved out for a while after the bank sold the building. I have had a very good relationship with the bank and in turn they sent me clients. My business grew because what I offered was pretty unusual. It was advice, not a product, not a dream to change your life. It was plain, simple advice based on the person, their life situation and their assets. With everyone else, if you asked them for advice, they wanted to sell you shares or managed funds.

In the early days of my advisory service, I had youth on my side and I wasn't afraid. I felt I had something to sell, that people would take it because nobody else was offering it. Through my experience with the stock exchange and broking, I knew what made people tick. I have a retired British surgeon as a neighbour at home. He walked into my bedroom one day when I was feeling unwell. He looked at me and said: 'You're dehydrated, you should be in hospital.'

'How do you know?' I said, taken aback.

'That's our training. I'm trained to look at the patient first, and make my assessment by just looking and talking to them. I know what's wrong with them.' The doctor was right. I had gone to a lunch and got salmonella poisoning. I'd had diarrhoea all night and all day. Within half an hour, he had me in hospital. And that's instinctively my training. That's what I try to do with finance; look at the whole person. I can assess people by talking to them for half an hour; I assess what makes them tick, their needs and objectives. It's the secret of my success.

An article in the *Sydney Morning Herald* (in 1986) captured my approach perfectly:

> Henri Aram prefers to call himself a 'financial psychiatrist'.
> 'Other people call themselves independent advisers but what they do is sell investment products – otherwise they don't eat. I prefer to assess a client's personality and gauge what types of investment he or she could handle emotionally.'

I felt very strongly about advisers whose real agenda was to sell the unsuspecting public a product they didn't need. 'I don't know of any independent investment advisers who are impartial,' I told David Koch in an article for *Business Review Weekly* (October 1982).

'The government should legislate for commissions to be disclosed on those products recommended by advisers, and also on any associations between dealer's representatives and investment companies.' (This was legislated in 2010.)

In those early days, the 1970s and 1980s, I would have appointments every hour. A lot of people who went to see me at the stock exchange advisory service then sought my advice when I was in private practice. It wasn't easy but I was fortunate enough to have my private income, my property investments, which supported the business for a while. Other people tried to follow in my footsteps but they were all commission-oriented, whereas my business was just straight advice. I've always said people can do better if they know how to do it themselves. Ultimately, this has been my secret in building up portfolios that people ultimately could manage by themselves.

ACROSS THE AIRWAVES

I never expected that my humble idea of giving people commonsense financial advice would be of any interest to the media. But once you plant the seed, you never know how big an idea can grow. To use financial jargon, I soon realised I could 'add value' to my stock exchange service. Together with Noel Adams, who I engaged as a publicity agent when I started private practice, I prepared a proposal to the Commonwealth Bank to support a Question and Answer segment on matters of personal finance on a radio program. The idea attracted the interest of the bank's CEO, Sir Bede Callaghan, and the segment was marketed to various stations before Sydney radio 2GB accepted it as part of Ian Parry-Okeden's nightly 10 pm program in 1975.

My segment was broadcast live for about 30 minutes from Monday to Friday. The host would ask me questions, and then listeners would also ring in with their own. The Commonwealth Bank, which sponsored the segment, advertised in the slots between my questions and answers.

The segment struck a chord with listeners, who had never been offered such direct access before to independent financial advice, and stayed on air much longer than I anticipated. This was helped in some part by the controversy over the Whitlam Government about whether to nationalise the banks. This heated climate attracted more listeners, and some dissent between me and the show's host.

The listeners showed their appreciation.

'This note is to congratulate you on your victory on air last night,' wrote Mrs MT, from Neutral Bay. 'Your direct speaking and knowledgeable arguments knocked down the Government speaker flat on his face. It was good to listen to.'

'I congratulate you most heartily on your stand against Socialism. Best of wishes and keep up your good work,' wrote Mr FH, from Sydney.

'May I say in all sincerity that for as long as there are forthright and good-thinking men like yourself still among us, our heritage and our freedom shall always be secure. Thank you again and God bless you,' wrote Mrs JF from Mosman.

One woman rang my office after a radio segment to ask a personal question. My secretary put her through and she asked coyly: 'Are you Jewish?'

Taken aback, I responded: 'Why do you ask?'

'I had an argument with my husband when I told him: "I bet he is Jewish to give such good advice".'

'You won!' I responded reluctantly.

The Whitlam Government's policies prompted several politicians to ring up as well. They saw the program as a free platform to put their views across. I had to be careful about what I said to them. If I overstepped the mark, the station had this button which immediately cut you off. The public wouldn't even know if you got cut off, because the advertisements would take over without even a blip. I think Parry-Okeden used it once in a debate about nationalisation of the banks. I can't prove it. But he certainly didn't agree with what I was saying. I made it clear that I didn't want any government interfering with my savings. That was about the only time I experienced any 'intervention'. In all my media work, I had a very good relationship with the owners, and never suffered any interference.

As is common with media comment, my segment often generated unintended reactions. One night the switchboard overloaded with calls after I finished. The calls were not about getting investment advice; they were from people objecting to cruelty to animals. The reason was that the Commonwealth Bank's advertisement said: 'If your kitchen is too small to swing a cat in, we will lend you the money to build a bigger kitchen.' I thought they were ringing up to ask for my advice, but they were ringing to complain. It took me a while, several callers, to realise what was going on.

Another time I received a call from Lady Violet Braddon, the widow of the prominent businessman Sir Henry Braddon. Lady Braddon had a beautiful home in Edgecliff Road, Edgecliff, and claimed the land tax was killing her. She wanted advice on how to combat the government, After my initial on-air response, I took up the fight on her behalf in my own time and we became personal friends. This indirectly led me into the political arena, which paved the way for my later election onto Woollahra Council in 1977.

The show was supposed to run for a couple of months and it proved a launching pad for a wide range of media over the next twenty years. I loved the cut and thrust of being on radio. Thanks to Dale Carnegie, I could answer fairly quickly. I enjoyed the banter and I made a lot of friends; enemies, too. The radio program also helped tremendously when I got on to the council because I was already a public figure. Radio is a very powerful medium. Over the years I was also invited onto the ABC Friday morning program, 'City Extra', with Caroline Jones on 2FC (now known as Radio National) and later, with Margaret Throsby.

The print media realised that plain advice on everyday family financial matters was perfect for newspapers and magazines – whose editors were desperate to find new features to promote to their readers. No one was doing it at the time so it was a strong selling point.

The first offer came late in 1975 from the *Sunday Telegraph*, which had been sold a few years earlier by the Packer empire to Rupert Murdoch's News Limited. My column was titled 'A Matter of Money' and it tapped the same need for basic, impartial information that my radio segment had touched. This media profile meant that my statements or opinions, which used to be fit for a few clients, suddenly became newsworthy. My scepticism about the Australian dream of buying your own home turned into a story in the *Sunday Telegraph* in 1976.

> A Sydney investment adviser wants a massive homes-for-rent building drive, using unused building materials and unemployed labour. Mr (Henri) Aram said this week young home-buyers were waking up to the fact that it was often cheaper to rent.
>
> 'The sooner young Australians get over their hang-up over home-ownership, the better,' he said. Mr Aram called on the Federal government to upgrade the image of rented accommodation and launch the building drive.
>
> He said: 'more and more young people with their feet firmly fixed on the ground no longer accept without question the outmoded concept of home ownership at all cost. Young people are turning away from prematurely buying their home because they are becoming more sophisticated in doing their sums correctly.'
>
> 'What people need are homes, not houses (and they should instead invest their savings productively rather than become mortgage slaves).'

My perspective, which now sounds slightly prophetic given the escalation of house prices since 2000, was based on commonsense but also on my European upbringing. People have been renting in Europe for centuries, the whole balance of household spending and saving is different from Australia because psychologically, they don't have an obsession with owning their own home. This frees them up to enjoy their life more, to pace their savings and mortgage years in order to build assets for both income and growth, and most importantly, to move to where the job opportunities arise.

My history of writing letters, which started with my father's court case over his camera during the war, now gained even greater currency thanks to my media profile. I burst into print whenever I saw injustice or excess, and the papers lapped it up. A typical example was the media's obsession with conspicuous profits, during a period of industrial unrest, which provoked me to write the following letter, which was printed in full by both the *Australian,* and then a week later, the *Sydney Morning Herald,* in May 1977.

> 'Profit' is the most misunderstood and abused word in our industrial language. Much of the communication atrophy (between employers and employees) results from the weakness in reporting financial data which over-emphasises the sensational and exposes itself to the practice of 'profit streaking' by those who seek to exploit it. The practice appears to have gone largely unnoticed.
>
> 'Streaking' is the flashlike exposure of a naked figure. As cricket enthusiasts well know, this can disrupt play. As it offends public decency, the practice has been outlawed.
>
> 'Profit streaking' is the sensational exposure of a naked profit figure. If it does not immediately offend decency, it does provide the

> more militant opponents of free enterprise with a powerful weapon with which to mislead the ignorant and disrupt industrial play.
>
> Nothing can be more destructive to industrial détente than the sensational publication of huge company profits or large interim profit increases denuded of their relationships to the amount of capital employed in achieving that result ...
>
> Free enterprise should insist that 'profit streakers' are discouraged from so exposing a naked figure of profit as to incite industrial disputation and disrupt the harmony of the game.

The late 1970s, of course, were also a time when streaking became highly popular at major cricket games. The term 'profit streaking' was immediately picked up by the media and entered the public lexicon.

In 1979 I received a phone call from Ita Buttrose, who was editor of the *Australian Women's Weekly*. Ita, as she is known to everyone, was the founding editor of *Cleo* magazine, which she launched a few years earlier, and had modern, fresh ideas about what women wanted to read about. As they gained more sexual and financial independence during the 1970s, Ita said, it was important for them to become more financially literate. Many had little or no understanding of even basic household financial matters and she wanted to help them become more self-reliant and able to debate these subjects with their men. Ita was a very charming woman, very intelligent, and of course, very close to Kerry Packer.

I could see the logic of her approach and I gladly accepted the offer to write for the *Weekly*. My first column was published in July 1979, under the headline: 'Henri Aram joins the Weekly with his … TAX GUIDE TO STOP YOU LOSING MONEY'. At the bottom, it ended with 'Henri Aram will appear in the Weekly with a regular guide to MONEY MATTERS'.

The *Weekly* gave me a lot of support throughout the ACP magazine network. My column ran for four years in the *Women's Weekly*, then occasionally in *Woman's Day* from 1983.

I always picked a subject of general interest, like tax minimisation. I delivered an article to them each week, which was actually quite stressful. To find something new each column is difficult, and you must also be aware that when you write about finance, if you mention a person or firm and you get your facts wrong you can be sued for a statement that may implicate them. Even getting a decimal point or fraction of a percentage wrong can lead to huge financial difficulties for any company named, and liabilities for the publishers. If you say a projected annual profit is $100 million instead of $10 million, or vice versa – simply by getting a zero wrong – you have instantly changed their status and image in the market; shares could be traded on the basis of your mistake.

Fortunately, that never happened. The column proved popular and I received strong feedback from ordinary readers. I had a box number at the GPO and it used to overflow with letters from people who wrote to me directly. Some of them came up with kooky ideas, such as the man who suggested I'd never written about gold in foreign banks.

My column at the *Women's Weekly* must have hit the spot because the *Sydney Morning Herald* offered me a column soon after. I wrote a weekly column for the *Herald* from 1981 to 1988, which led to a number of other speaking jobs. One of these was with Ross Gittins, then an economics writer, and now the esteemed economics editor of the *Sydney Morning Herald*. In the 1980s we gave a seminar at the Centrepoint tower which drew 1500 people there. One woman wanted some advice: her house and garden had appreciated in value. What would be my recommendation?

'Tell me one thing. Do you enjoy your garden?' I asked.

'I only have the house because of the garden – I love gardening,' she replied.

'Why would you want to sell it for profit? What would you do with the money?' I shot back. And everyone clapped.

When I started my own business, I used to hire the conference room at Australia Square. I conducted seminars and 300–400 people would attend. I always tried to give commonsense advice. 'If you enjoy the use of whatever the money does, then that's a good investment.' People enjoy giving to charity. I give a lot to charity, not because I'm a charitable person but because I get a kick out of helping others. People have different ideas about what gives them enjoyment. If you can enjoy what money brings you, it's the best investment you can make. I call it psychic income. And psychic income doesn't attract tax. That's always been my philosophy. Psychic income is the enjoyment of your money. So far, they haven't found a way of taxing it! During a Q&A session on the effects of compounding interest, a young lady – having been asked how much she would need to take off if offered $20,000 less 12 per cent – pondered before replying coyly: 'Everything bar my earrings, I suppose.'

The *Herald* also put me in touch with a younger audience. In September 1982 the paper ran a story about a twelve-year-old boy from North Turramurra on Sydney's North Shore, who wanted to be a millionaire at 21. His name was Murray Winton and he had received a letter from BHP saying it could not accept his $200 savings as shares. It was uneconomical for the company to accept his money and he needed a bigger parcel of shares to start a portfolio.

I read the article, got in touch with a stockbroking firm, bought 250 shares, and told the broker: 'Book 50 to this young boy, and 200 for me.' The next day, the paper wrote a follow-up story under the headline, 'Murray is on his way to that $m':

> Murray Winton, the Sydney schoolboy who wanted to invest his hard-earned savings in BHP shares, had his dream come true yesterday.
>
> Investment adviser Henri Aram, a regular columnist in the *Herald*'s Personal Finance section on Tuesdays, filled Murray's order for 20 BHP shares yesterday morning. The shares were purchased as part of a larger parcel through a nominee company, thus avoiding the minimum level rule.
>
> 'It's just a matter of spending a little time helping a small investor,' Mr Aram said. 'I'm surprised more stockbrokers don't do this sort of thing.'

In all my columns, or financial advice, I wanted to be there for the ordinary person, for commonsense. Ordinary people were too small for the banks, who would put them into bonds. Banks didn't buy shares in those days for people. They only had managed funds, and their money was peanuts. But I've always believed that people should build their own portfolio, where they get their rights entitlement (to new share issues) and their bonus, after which they can reinvest the dividends. They can do better than any managed fund.

My public profile flourished in the *Herald*. In August 1986, the paper carried a feature article about trustworthiness, which included interviews with a broad range of well-known media figures to examine what made someone earn the public's trust. I was one of them.

> Two trusted financial advisers, Henri Aram and Bruce Bond, also provide living evidence of the reliability of their advice.
>
> Neither would reveal their incomes but both suggested they

were reasonably well off. Henri Aram said he did not earn much from his advisory business and both men said they did their jobs mainly for the satisfaction of helping the public.

They both attribute the trust bestowed on them to long careers of giving sound advice. They both claim they are trusted because they don't stand to profit personally from people following their advice.

A media profile also brought with it some awkward spin-offs. When I went out to dinner or a show, people would pump me for information. If I sat down to dinner, the person next to me would bypass the small talk. 'What do you think of the market?' My stock standard answer to this was, and remains: 'It will continue to fluctuate.' Often it felt like they were talking to me to learn something rather than converse. People think you have inside information, which you don't. I never encouraged inside information, never acted on rumours. I acted on my own readings. All my life, I've always read the daily press, I do this maybe at the expense sometimes of my family life. It's often been said to me: 'You're always reading the papers, why don't you talk to me?' If you enjoy what you're doing, the reading is not a task. It's part of my daily life. I've done it for years.

In 1988 the *Herald* restructured and the *Weekend Australian* came to the party; my column moved there from 1989 to 1997. Meanwhile, I had branched out into books, again courtesy of Noel Adams, who saw the benefits of me being in print and on radio at the time, and pushed me to start writing. The first book, titled *Money Matters*, combined all the advice I had dispensed in my columns into a single, easy-to-read guide, written in language everyone could understand. It was published under the ABC imprint in 1982, while I was appearing on the Caroline Jones radio program, and contained a foreword by Sir Roden Cutler, the Governor of NSW.

I believe that financial and economic factors are not understood by the majority of the community. We are all faced, sooner or later, with decisions which involve personal budgeting, investments, taxation and business and commercial law.

Mr Aram in his book gives a very practical and lucid dissertation on such matters under simple and easy to find headings To use the author's own words, the book 'promotes nothing but common sense'.

One of the features that set this book apart from others was that it addressed women and their management of money. Through my radio talkback, newspaper and *Women's Weekly* columns in particular, I had come to appreciate the special issues that confronted women – from the young and single, to middle-age and widowhood.

'One way for a single girl to learn a lot about money quickly is to get to know a millionaire bachelor! Failing that, there is no reason why a woman should not be able to manage her financial affairs as competently as any man. Many of them do in fact, some even eminently better,' my chapter titled *Money and the Single Woman* began.

'Seven out of ten Australian wives outlive their husbands. The chance that your own wife may survive you and become a widow should never be too far from any husband's mind. Widowhood, when it comes, can add a money crisis to the problems of a woman already stricken with grief,' I wrote in a later chapter, *Preparation for Widowhood.* 'Every husband should ask himself: "How well has my wife been prepared for an event that may strike when least expected?" Today men die younger and often quite suddenly. The high incidence of heart disease and stress-related illnesses and increasing road tolls leave younger widows with the obligation of a young family. Many are unprepared to cope emotionally and financially with the problems ahead.'

The chapter on widowhood was, in particular, noted by reviewers and commentators, and I was given the nickname of 'The Widow's Friend', which I took in the best sense of the term.

Looking back, when this book was published in 1982, women had already started to live more independently on their own terms, thanks to the breakthroughs of the 1960s and early 1970s. But the impact of the groundbreaking reform of divorce laws in 1975 had not yet unfolded. If I was to rewrite the book today, I would add a chapter about women and divorce, and perhaps another on managing your life afterwards. These two experiences are now commonplace for many, if not a majority, of Australian women and provide an ongoing burden in their lives.

Money Matters sold so well that in 1985 an updated edition was published by Allen & Unwin. It eventually went on to sell nearly 100,000 copies. When the stock market crashed two years later, in 1987, I started work on a second book called *Money Matters More,* because so many people had lost their money, and the little they had left, I thought, 'matters a lot more, because people have to understand how to be careful with it'.

It was published in 1993 (again by Allen & Unwin) and Ita Buttrose, who snapped me up as a columnist at the *Women's Weekly* in the 1970s, did another story on me in her recently launched magazine, titled *Ita.* She sent the well-known journalist Dorian Wild to interview me. This is how he started his article:

The newspapers are full of gloom and doom: unemployment has

never been higher and stories on the economy make you want to slash your wrists. But in his 5th floor office in the middle of the Sydney CBD, financial adviser Henri Aram puts on a happy face.

'It's important to be positive,' he says. 'Take being retrenched – it could be your lucky day!' He notes my startled expression. 'I mean it,' he adds. 'If you are in your forties and you receive a payout of $100,000, it could be the ideal moment to set up your own business. Being retrenched can be the start of a new and wonderful career!'

The great thing about Henri Aram is that he's such a reassuring guy. Just when you're thinking there's no way in the world you can ever manage your money effectively, Aram is there with his bedside manner, talking a lot of commonsense.

IF YOU CAN'T BEAT 'EM ...

In 1970 I had bought a property called Knowle on New South Head Road in Double Bay, from a member of the prominent Sydney law firm, Allen, Allen and Hemsley. You couldn't live in it at the time – the roof was half off and needed complete replacement. Soon after the documents were exchanged, I received a land tax enquiry from the Land Tax Office.

'Is the property owner occupied?' it asked.

I should have answered simply, yes. But I was too honest. Instead, I wrote: 'The property is now owner occupied to the extent that it needs repairs – but it is not habitable. Now in the process of renovation.' So the Tax Office sent me a land tax assessment for around $3000, which was a fortune at that time. I objected strongly, had numerous exchanges with the Tax Office and even wrote to the then Liberal Premier, Sir Robert Askin, offering to pay the money to a charity rather than paying to the tax office, just to spite them. Askin refused, explaining it as follows: 'The property is not subject to land tax if it's owner occupied.' I wrote 'property vacant'. That was the difference. I learned my lesson – when you get these forms, you should stretch the truth just a little or else you pay for it.

This raised my hackles and cost me quite a bit of unnecessary money but it paled into insignificance compared to the battle I was to have with Woollahra Council over its 'minimum rating' policy – which eventually propelled me into local government. The property next door to Knowle, which had a tennis court, submitted a development application to knock down the house and build a high-rise apartment block, Colebrook, in its place. The council had approved the application on the condition that the high-rise was set back by the width of the tennis court and the ceding of one parking lot on my property, a concrete slab 2.5 metres x 5 metres. When I got my first rate notice from the Woollahra Council, it assessed the parking lot as a separate property with minimum rates, and assessed the main house with about six bedrooms at virtually the same rate as the parking lot.

I was outraged and wrote to the council again: 'The property should be combined for rating purposes.' They refused, saying it was considered a separate lot; it had not been consolidated.

Throughout my life, I have always been motivated by principle. If I see something wrong or unfair, I will fight it. I did so with financial matters – whether it affected an industry or ordinary people. This time there was only one victim: me. I refused to pay the rates, and I followed my instincts, as my father did 35 years earlier, when he was challenged over his camera.

I took the council to court. It was June 1976, and the *Sydney Morning Herald* was there to cover the case.

> A householder facing a rates bill of almost $350 for 'a slab of concrete' claimed in court yesterday that Woollahra Council was discriminating against him. But the court found for the council and ordered Mr Henri Aram to pay the rates and court costs.
>
> [Mr Aram] said that residents in the block of flats [next to him] had similar garages to his but were not required to pay a separate rate. He had put the matter to the State Government Minister

> involved, who had indicated the council could use its discretion on consolidating properties for rating purposes.
>
> Mr Aram said: 'I have asked the council on repeated occasions to use their discretion and they say it is not their policy. I do not think the law is applied in good conscience and I think the council is discriminating against me.'

The judge was sympathetic: 'I'm afraid you have a good cause, but we cannot intervene in council matters,' he wrote in his judgment. 'If I were you, if you can't beat them, join them.'

Still outraged, I contacted Syd Einfeld, the then NSW Minister for Consumer Affairs in the Wran Labor Government. 'This is an injustice for the average person. How are they going to pay a minimum rate for a garage?' I wrote.

Einfeld and I had known each other for several years, courtesy of several exchanges in the papers about traffic accidents on New South Head Road. My house was on a long bend and cars would come down the road too fast, often skidding when it was wet. There were dozens of accidents and three or four people were actually killed when their vehicles went into my garage. After the last fatality, I wrote in the papers that it was criminal negligence, which prompted the council to finally build a median strip. However, in the process they moved a light pole right in front of the entrance, between the garage and the entrance. But the council forgot I was in the process of rebuilding the garage. I couldn't have the light pole moved and the original entrance to my property, which was heritage-listed, had to be altered.

Einfeld was as a good as his word, and took the matter up with Harry Jensen, the Minister for Local Government. Jensen wrote to Einfeld:

> The issue raised by Mr Aram is not capable of easy solution as the Woollahra Municipal Council has not been prepared to take

> advantage of Ministerial undertakings which would permit some relief being granted to Mr Aram by combining the assessment in respect of his car parking space with that relating to his residence.

Predictably, the government didn't do anything, although Einfeld was courteous enough to let me know:

> The Minister for Local Government has expressed concern at this situation as well as a number of other aspects of local government rating ... Nevertheless, it would appear that I am not in a position to be of any further assistance to you.

After the court case the council confirmed that it would not budge, although it did send a committee to inspect the garage at Colebrook (next door), which provided rear access to my property. The Mayor, Alderman Backhouse, came with the others on a bus to inspect the parking lot. I came out to introduce myself. 'I'd like to make representation,' I said. 'When we need you, we'll call you,' Alderman Backhouse said abruptly, and they continued their inspection without me. Shortly after the inspection, they did call me. 'I'm sorry, it's too late now, because I'm off to the office,' I replied.

That was a turning point. I saw that the council did not care about ordinary people, and when I wrote to the papers about my experience I received widespread support. 'You should stand as an independent for the council,' people said. The idea appealed to me, and even more to Tina. It was not about power or public office. It was the opportunity to help, to improve life for others and to remedy unfair practices.

For the record, the NSW government eventually took up my complaint and capped the minimum rating policy at a more reasonable level.

OTHER FISH TO FRY

I was eager to get into council and take up the battle against stupidity and waste. But first I had other fish to fry. In the middle of my battle with Woollahra Council, I launched another campaign – to promote the image of the lowly carp for human consumption. In early 1976 the *Sydney Morning Her*ald published an article that the government was going to spend $2 million to eradicate the European carp because of the damage it was causing native fish and river plant life. The fish was tainted with the reputation of having a muddy taste because it favours river embankments, the article claimed. However, I was quite familiar with the carp from my childhood. There would be a carp swimming in the bathtub of most European homes every Christmas and New Year. I knew from my childhood that it didn't need to be eradicated. Certainly, the carp has a lot of bones. But properly prepared, it was a nourishing dish.

I launched my campaign because I could see a waste of a very valuable resource, which struck a nerve. The government was planning to spend millions of dollars to eradicate a fish that could feed many thousands. I knew it could be commercially viable and I thought it was a waste of taxpayers' money to get rid of it rather than using it to feed the poor.

I wrote a letter to the paper in reply to the article, in which I said that even the most delicate of palates will develop taste for carp.

> Your article made only brief reference to the fact that European migrants regarded the carp as a delicacy. This is not confined to migrants; anyone that has travelled Europe and tasted the many exquisite ways in which carp dishes can be served will testify that it is more than a mere delicacy – it is a rare culinary experience.
>
> Even palates nurtured on the delicacies of meat pie with tomato sauce will readily adapt to the taste of carp with butter sauce. At 40 cents a kilo say for carp (compared with around $2.50 a pound for John Dory) the hip pocket nerves of every housewife will soon stimulate the nerves of the palate should this be necessary at all.
>
> If you can't beat them, EAT them.

Predictably, that turned into a slogan for my campaign. A month later Tina and I organised a carp banquet at our house to prove the point, calling on our wide range of friends in Sydney's business and social networks. I found a Romanian woman who had a number of recipes for the fish. The papers were invited and lapped it up. In February 1977, the *Sun-Herald* reported:

> Members of Sydney's social set and international gourmets got together at a garden banquet at Double Bay one day this week – and feasted on the common carp. And most agreed it was delicious.
>
> Guests at the carp party included Sir Percy Spender, former Justice of the International Court at the Hague and Ambassador to Washington, Mrs Leon Myerson, a past president of the Black and White society, Mrs Adele Aldritt, Mr and Mrs Herbert de Graff, Mrs Diana Von Kohorn, Mr Oliver Shaul, director of Summit

> restaurants. (The journalist George Negus also attended, and took home the leftovers for his daughter's 21st birthday.)
>
> Romanian-born Mrs Cherry Orly prepared the dishes with the assistance of her husband. Mrs Orly said: 'You might call us carpologists.'
>
> Mr Aram said he would like to see some recipes for carp made available to the public. He said: 'Perhaps they could be sold for a dollar and the proceeds given to the Freedom for Hunger Appeal.'

A few weeks later the NSW Committee of the Freedom from Hunger Campaign wrote to me to thank me for my suggestion and confirmed that they would be willing to cooperate with any such promotion.

My banquet had an immediate impact, which was recognised in NSW Parliament with a question (in March) in the Upper House by Peter Philips, MLC:

> Is the government spending large sums of taxpayers' money on a programme to eliminate European carp from our rivers and lakes? Is the Minister [for Planning and Environment] aware that the carp could make a protein-rich, delectable food at a low price?
>
> Is the Minister aware, also, that the price of carp jumped from 60c a pound earlier this year to 80c on 18th February, with a further rise to $1.20 a pound four days after the carp had received favourable publicity in the *Sun-Herald* on 20th February?
>
> What can the minister do to ensure adequate supplies of this fish at the lowest possible price to the harassed housewife?

Beyond changing the market value of carp almost overnight because of the interest my banquet attracted, I received a lot of recipes from people in Tasmania who were already preparing and eating carp. I told them that in Asia in the rainy season when they can't grow rice, they breed carp in the rice paddies for human consumption. I wrote to several ministers in the Federal government as part of my campaign, and received replies from three (including John Howard and Ian Sinclair) who all politely pointed out alleged environmental problems that it posed. I also met strong resistance from the Doyle family, who owned the famous seafood restaurant at Rose Bay (now at Watson Bay). Mr Doyle disputed whether the carp was suitable for consumption.

Like many of my ideas, this was one was ahead of its time. More than twenty years later, the prominent Australian chef Matthew Moran, among a group of leading chefs, gave his endorsement to the carp. In July 1997 the *Herald* gave it a big run, under the headline, 'Cooks urge us to stop carping and east the pest':

> According to the Sydney chef Matthew Moran, owner of the Potts Point restaurant Moran's, carp (a close cousin of the goldfish) is a perfectly edible fish that suffers from a huge image problem.
>
> 'When it was first suggested to me to cook carp I just screwed my nose up at it,' Mr Moran said. 'I've always considered it a pest and inedible. However, I was wrong. It's got a slightly earthy flavour to it, but with the right recipe it's quite a good fish.'
>
> Yesterday Mr Moran helped to launch a new carp cookbook by preparing two dishes for a gathering of food writers and critics.
>
> The cookbook launch is part of a campaign by the NSW Government to get carp on dining tables and help control the spread of the fish, an introduced species which has infested our waterways since the '70s.
>
> The idea to eat carp arose during a carp fishing competition in Tamworth earlier this year conducted by the NSW Department of Land and Water Conservation.
>
> A recipe competition was held to generate ideas for using the carp caught in the competition.

'The competition revealed there were a lot of closet carp eaters out there,' a Land and Water Conservation officer, Mr Col Easton, said.

'Considering it is the world's most widely eaten fish, it is surprising that Australians have looked down on it for so long. It is a cheap fish in this country, so its potential is huge.'

Carp is classified as a noxious pest in most States and has been blamed for wreaking havoc on native fish stocks and inland water quality.

The species has also made its presence felt in urban areas.

During a four-day clean out of the Centennial Park ponds in March, three tonnes of carp were caught and used as fertiliser. The largest fish weighed 13.5 kilograms.

Peter Doyle could not restrain himself in this letter to the paper in reply:

> Heaven forbid if we have reached the stage where we are forced to eat this earthy, bony heap of dung.

I may have lost the battle, but in the end I feel that I won the carp war.

Leading chef Matt Moran holding a carp (1997), which I fought a long campaign to make edible during the 1970s (Photo courtesy Fairfax Syndication Services)

BIRTH OF AN ALDERMAN

I stood as an independent for the Double Bay Ward of Woollahra Council in the 1977 local government elections. Woollahra was, and still is, one of the most affluent municipalities in Australia, full of glitzy harbourfront mansions and large, leafy blocks built with old money. It covers some of the most famous postcodes in the country – Darling Point, Point Piper, Vaucluse, Bellevue Hill, Paddington, and of course, Double Bay. The residents paid a lot of money to live in these suburbs and they exerted a lot of pressure on the council when they wanted to develop or improve their propensities, or felt that somebody else's plans might compromise their million-dollar views. With my investment planning, media work, a young daughter and an active social life, the idea of campaigning and marketing myself was daunting, but Tina pushed me. We had met a lot of people in the Eastern Suburbs community through her involvement in the Black and White Committee, and through my business connections. When we floated the idea that I would stand, I was surprised at how much support there was for me. Tina was my de facto campaign manager; she loved electioneering. It came naturally to her, tapping into the same organisational and lobbying skills she employed on the social scene.

My campaign slogan was simple: 'Better government, fairer for the small people'. It reflected who I was and what I cared about: reform, fairness, modest but committed activism. The campaign flyer had the following, clear direct messages:

I am AGAINST:
The amalgamation of local councils
Waste of taxpayer's money
Party politics in local councils
Extravagance of any form, and red tape

I am FOR:
Rationalisation between councils of cost-intensive services
A just apportionment of the rate burden without discrimination (in short, a fairer rating system and a reduction in the minimum rate)
Honest and responsible government, a 'Fair Go' for all peoples in the community, be they residents, shopkeepers or ratepayers.

As an independent I was up against a powerful opposition: the Woollahra Action Committee (WAC), full of wealthy businessmen, had been the dominant force on the council for years. Some of the group were rattled by my campaign. At one point Tina overheard a fellow from the Woollahra Action Committee, Ces Monkhouse, talking to a local resident as he was handing out how-to-vote leaflets: 'Don't vote for this fellow, he's not only a foreigner, he's also a Jew.' Tina confronted him: 'How dare you!' she began. The resident was just as outraged: 'I wouldn't vote for you if you were the last man standing.'

The campaign also contained some pleasant surprises. While handing out my how-to-vote cards at St Mark's Hall in Darling Point, a lady walked up and I handed her my ticket. Her face was familiar. 'I know you from somewhere,' I said, puzzled.

'They all say that,' she shot back.

She came out of the polling booth and talked to me again: 'I did vote for you, although I don't know you.'

'But I know you ... what's your name?'

'Bryant.'

'Is that your married name? What's your maiden name?'

'It's Stanger. Jean Stanger.'

A look of recognition came over her. 'You're not young Henri, are you?'

I nodded sheepishly. I hadn't heard that expression for 40 years.

Jean Stanger was Major Murray Jones' secretary all those years ago at de Havilland; she was the first person I met there and she was responsible for all the Major's correspondence on my behalf. Jean voted for me (and sent me a warm letter of congratulations when I was elected) and later became my client; I enabled her to live very comfortably for the rest of her life.

The Action Committee played dirty as a group, too. Traditionally their how-to-vote forms were blue and the ALP candidates' were pink, so I made my voting paper yellow – for independent. Lo and behold, on election day the Action Committee, which had put me last on their ticket, handed out yellow forms to confuse voters and eat into my vote. It didn't make any difference. I got more votes than the Mayor. I was almost as shocked at the result as they were. I was the first independent to ever break through against them. I published a public letter of thanks to everyone who voted for me, and worked for me. I ended the message with a special thankyou to Tina: 'To my wife – the one and only spark plug in my Party Machine!'

Once the excitement died down, the reality of council life was punishing. First there were the committee meetings, mainly at night, and several nights a week. It was relentless. In the full council meetings I was declared a Labor stooge by the Action Committee. They joked about me: 'Council now has a full house. The Mayor was Backhouse, her deputy was Monkhouse and now we have shithouse [Aram],' was a quote cheekily concocted about me. I wore it with pride.

There was plenty of needling but I was enthusiastic and wouldn't be easily shut up. The debate was often heated and antagonistic. However, I had two supporters among the council's committee members. One was George Warnecke, a Labor man who had never been tipped out. The other was David Bitel, a solicitor. That meant there were three of us who could oppose the Action Committee, who held the other twelve seats.

As is common in politics, however, personal rapport often bridges the widest of political divides. During the election campaign I met Sir Neville Pixley, the businessman and president of the Action Committee from 1977 to 1980. Despite standing on different sides of the political divide, we hit it off when I introduced myself, though he held himself back because he couldn't be seen to be over-friendly with me because of his position on the Action Committee. Some years later Sir Neville's daughter put in an application to extend her home, and the council's building committee – comprised of aldermen and council staff such as engineers and town planners – decided to reject the extension, mainly due to antagonism to Sir Neville's profile. 'Why should his daughter be given preference?' they muttered.

When council committees consider applications, their decisions are then put before the full council at its fortnightly meetings, where they are usually rubber-stamped. After the building committee unanimously decided to refuse this particular development application, I took the liberty of ringing Sir Neville: 'I'm the independent, and not a great friend of the Action Committee, but I thought I'd let you know the matter comes before the council tonight, and is likely to be refused. I don't want to tell you the details, but I think if you came along ...'

Sir Neville took the hint. That night he turned up in his best suit and sat in the front of the public gallery where every alderman could see him. When the application came before council, I stood up and moved for approval. There was no shortage of seconders. Nobody dared to oppose it because they were scared of crossing him to his face, and of the retribution that would follow. Politicians find it easy to say no when someone is absent, but when it came to sticking their necks out and putting names to their votes they didn't have the guts. Sir Neville rang me the next day to thank me. He knew the scale of the favour I had done for him, and I made an important political ally.

I made plenty of enemies, too. One of them was a friend who was in a social crowd I mixed with at Nielsen Park, in Vaucluse. His son submitted an application to build a tennis court, which the council approved, subject to retention of trees. When this man built the tennis court, he ignored the council's condition and cut all the trees down. A year or two later, he applied to fit night lights around the tennis court, which was wedged in between a cluster of two or three properties. Because he had illegally cleared the trees the first time, the building committee indicated that it was likely to oppose this second application. The father asked me to speak on his son's behalf.

'I haven't made up my mind on this yet, and a lot of people approached me – adjoining owners – saying it's unfair to have tennis court lights outside their bedrooms,' I told him bluntly. They took that as a diplomatic way of telling them I was on their side but could not be seen to have prejudged the matter. When the application formally came before council, the whole family sat in the gallery, expecting me to speak up in favour of the plan. I voted against the lights. They looked daggers at me and none of them ever spoke to me again.

As an independent, I could not be forced to vote as part of a bloc, which meant I was viewed as a target who could be pressured. This sometimes bordered on harassment and intimidation. My home had a letterbox at the street level, but it was not used; mail was delivered through Colebrook, the house next door. Once there was a residents' petition which I did not receive until I came home from the meeting at which the petition was to be presented because it had been left in the downstairs letterbox and not in my upstairs letterbox. The residents rounded on me for not presenting the petition to council.

Although council was hectic, I still had energy for other campaigns in the business world. Foremost among these was my one-man effort in 1979 to save the Bank of Adelaide, with which I had enjoyed a happy relationship ever since my early days as a stockbroker with the Adelaide firm, Cutten and Harvey. My premises in George Street are in a building that was owned by the Bank of Adelaide and their head office, which gave me the first lease.

The bank had got into funding difficulties through its affiliate company, the Finance Corporation of Australia (FCA), which overextended on real estate transactions. I was concerned that the Bank of Adelaide may be forced to merge and lose its unique identity as a medium-sized bank. I took my complaint right to the top and wrote to the Prime Minister, Malcolm Fraser, proposing a merger with the Banque Nationale de Paris, which already had a presence in Australia, and a similar status. But the government rejected my proposal; the senior ministers weren't keen on allowing foreign banking to gain a stronger foothold in Australia.

At least I received a formal reply from the then Treasurer, John Howard, explaining why my idea had been knocked back in favour of a merger with the ANZ.

Dear Alderman Aram,
I have carefully considered what you have said and fully understand your concern ...

With regard to your comment about the opportunity for foreign banks to make an offer for the shares of the Bank of Adelaide, I have already told Federal Parliament that the Government has an open mind as to whether or not the long-standing policy in this area should continue in the future.

However, the fact remains the Board of Directors of the Bank of Adelaide has decided to recommend to the bank's shareholders approval of a merger with the ANZ Banking group. I have indicated my approval in principle to that merger. It is ultimately a matter for the shareholders of the Bank of Adelaide to determine the fate of the merger proposal.

Yours sincerely,
John Howard

In due course they merged and the Bank of Adelaide name went into oblivion, as I had feared. I do, however, cherish a commemorative silver cup inscribed 'To Henri Aram, from your Bank of Adelaide friends – 30th May, 1986'.

I stood for council at two more elections. In 1980 I secured 1373 out of 5556 voters, the second highest total, and my then running mate Jan Nyhan received 656 primary votes, which meant my ticket got 40 per cent of the primary vote. Three years later, in 1983, I tallied almost as many votes, 1345 out of a smaller total of 4930 voters, and was returned for my third – and what was to be final – term on the council.

By this time my profile as an independent, together with my media work, led to me being approached on several occasions to enter State politics. In hindsight I'm glad I never went down that path. Perhaps the most surprising offer came on behalf of the Catholic politician, Bob Santamaria, who asked me through one of his deputies to join the Democratic Labor Party, the DLP, which he founded in the 1950s following a split with the Australian Labor Party. I declined. 'I've got my own problems, and quite frankly, State politics is not on my radar at the moment,' I replied to his messenger. Santamaria said he asked me because he was impressed with my attitude to people, on radio and in my writings. Even to this day people come up to me and say: 'I remember you from the radio.' Somehow, people took to my voice, which has tended to be calm, measured. I think people found me reasoned and reassuring.

Besides, there was more than enough to keep me busy in Woollahra. I campaigned on a platform of fighting waste and excess, and the council gave me plenty of ammunition. In 1980, the Mayor, Alderman Charles Widdy, chose a $45,000 Mercedes-Benz as his mayoral car, and I told the council he should replace it with a less expensive alternative. It was a sheer waste of money. 'The council had $45,000 tied up when it could be invested at 12 per cent,' I told the council, according to a report in the *Wentworth Courier* on 6 November. 'It was not a good investment retaining the car because the council was losing up to $6000 a year in interest which could be gained from the money being invested. This cost must be added to the costs and there are also the wages of a chauffeur.'

Of course, my motion was lost on the voices. Amazingly, the council continued to flaunt its wastage on the mayoral car for years. I attacked again, as the *Courier* report in April 1984 demonstrates:

> Despite a protest by one alderman, Woollahra Council is to buy a current model Mercedes-Benz 280 SE Automatic saloon at a total cost of $50,412.20, including registration. The car will replace the current Mercedes-Benz as the mayoral vehicle.
> At the recent council meeting when the matter was tabled, Ald. Henri Aram tried to move an amendment that the council accept the tender for a (locally produced) Ford LTD sedan at $21,100, excluding registration.
>
> He said it would be a sheer waste of ratepayers' money to buy an imported vehicle for a difference of $25,000. Ald. Aram said he was not sure the Mayor needed a Mercedes-Benz. Ratepayers might be just as happy to see him driving around in a locally-produced chauffeur-driven Ford.
> There was no seconder for Ald. Aram's amendment.

In August 1986, in the face of continued wasteful spending, I proposed that the council relinquish the Mercedes, hot dinners, liquor and imported mineral water ... and invest the savings in a welfare fund for the needy in the municipality. The *Courier* reported the matter.

> Ald. Aram said he shared the compassion some aldermen had expressed about the welfare of the underprivileged, and believed the council should examine its own expenditures before funding welfare services.
> 'If we are sincere we should look at the welfare situation.'
> Ald. Aram's motion was lost, only three aldermen supporting it.

I did score a few victories over the years and one of my favourites came in 1981, when the council had to decide who to send to the annual Local Government Conference, to be held that year in Port Macquarie on the mid-north coast. The fifteen aldermen – twelve from WAC, David Bitel and George Warnecke (Labor) and myself (independent) – sat around discussing who we would elect as our representative. The mood was relaxed, slightly nonchalant, and most of my colleagues barely paid attention to the discussion, assuming that we would once again send someone from the WAC. It was just a question of whose turn it was.

On an impulse, and to test how alert they were, I decided to propose that David Bitel be Woollahra's representative. Woollahra was a staunchly Liberal municipality and had never elected a Labor representative. Without thinking, Alderman David Joel seconded the motion. The WAC had not caucused beforehand, so suddenly the room was filled with confusion as they all contemplated this bizarre situation. Left to think for themselves, with everyone watching each other and too embarrassed to reject him one by one, they voted eight out of fifteen to endorse Bitel as the representative. Alderman Frank Donoghue, the influential head of the Vaucluse Ward group, stormed out of the room furious, taking his Vaucluse group with him.

The upshot of this vote was twofold: A Labor alderman represented Woollahra for the first time and, more significantly, the WAC splintered, as Donoghue and his followers split from the other WAC members. Eventually, it led to the disintegration of the Woollahra Action Committee as a political force on the council.

Getting the better of aldermen was child's play compared to dealing with residents' harbour views and privacy, especially when it came to trees. Of all the local problems that got under people's skins in Woollahra, trees were perhaps the most difficult. It was hardly surprising, given how many and how old some of them were. I had a personal encounter with trees before council and I had many more as an alderman; my inclination was to protect the interests of people who wanted to protect trees. Although they aroused strong passions right across the city, people got very heated over them in the Eastern Suburbs when they outlaid huge sums for their large, leafy properties. In the 1960s, there was a tree at the top of Ocean Avenue and New South Head Road, in Edgecliff, which was removed by council for a road-widening project. The whole council was tipped out at the next election over the removal of that tree.

The tree problem came even closer to home. My house in Double Bay had a huge Moreton Bay fig in front of it, higher than the property itself on the street frontage. This had been a landmark for many years but also made the front rooms excessively dark. It could not be trimmed or cut because of the expected public outcry. However, nature intervened when the roots destroyed the concrete sewerage line from Fairfax Road behind the block, leaving dozens of properties without this service. Council was forced to remove the tree as a matter of urgency, much to the dismay of locals. The other problem on this site came from two magnificent jacarandas at the rear boundary, where the colourful flower display was the pride and joy of adjoining Colebrook residents. When a new owner moved in, the trees suddenly died an unnatural death and I was left with the arduous task of removing the stumps. Although the trees had been clearly poisoned, council refused to investigate because the Tree Preservation Act stated that a person must be identified for a prosecution to occur – an impossible and virtually unenforceable provision as anyone poisoning a tree would do so unobserved. This was a widespread problem in all municipalities.

People take council decisions very personally when it comes to their properties. On Vaucluse Road, past Kincoppal Catholic School and leading to Nielsen Park, there was a property whose owners applied to the council for two dormer windows to be built into the roof. The people behind objected on the grounds it would have blocked a tiny fraction of their view. I was approached by the objectors ahead of the decision. 'Look, I can't really see that it's going to make all that much difference,' I told them. I was overruled; the dormer windows were refused. Within a couple of years, two huge trees that had been planted on either side of the house totally blocked the view of the people who had objected to the dormer windows. The property is still there, so are the trees. Nobody could enter it to remove the trees, because that would be illegal entry. People become very vindictive, and shrewd, in their vengeance.

Being in the firing line of these decisions, I made a lot of enemies and a lot of friends. Often, I was subtly reminded of the fact that I was a Jew and a foreigner – you never lived it down. People would make suggestions and intimidate you whichever way they could. My mother was dead against me standing for council because she always believed that, being Jewish, I shouldn't expose myself or become vulnerable. I was determined to live that down – I wasn't going to let anyone dictate to me if I felt an injustice was being done. I do this to this very day. My mother came to be proud of what I was doing on council, though she didn't like me being exposed because of our experience in Germany. When Hitler came to power, people in government or local government positions were among the first to be liquidated.

Local government regulations could be extremely frustrating when you tried to innovate. I campaigned for the introduction of footpath restaurants – al fresco dining. A Frenchman came on to the council from the Action Committee. 'In Paris there are boulevards where people sit out in the street, the climate here is ideal,' he argued. Now I had an accomplice. But there was no way we could get the proposal approved. The full-time staff, the Town Clerk and other bureaucrats said it was against the regulations. People had to stick within the four walls of their shop. Eventually they relaxed the rules, when other municipalities had taken the lead. The ultimate authority always lay with the Town Clerk. Whatever he recommended, the Mayor had to go along with. That's why it takes a lot of effort to change the bureaucratic set of rules and regulations.

With so much at stake, and so many rich, powerful residents, the stain of corruption occasionally reared its ugly head. I never saw any evidence of corruption among the council's full-time staff. But what was presented sometimes in council committees – that's another matter. Although I never saw brown paper bags, people were not afraid to use whatever means they could to persuade aldermen. For example, when I first stood for council I received a cheque for a large amount of money from a company to help me in my electioneering. There was no introduction, just the money. I sent the cheque back. While it is possible that corruption did take place, I can't say I have any positive knowledge of it. However, some decisions didsurprise me. There's a tall building opposite Edgecliff train station, on the corner of Darling Point Road, a high-rise building which now has an extra four storeys on it. There was a lot of discussion about that at the time. They got their four additional storeys.

Among the whirlwind of my council duties, business and newspaper columns, I let myself be talked into standing on a ticket for election to the board of the NRMA motoring group. In 1986, David Parker –

an economist, flamboyant personality and former mayor of Woollahra Council – asked me to join his group of eight prominent figures to throw out the existing board. Parker, who was an NRMA director at the time, assembled a group that included Ted Mack, the Mayor of North Sydney, Roger Dunlop, a doctor and former president of the Australian Medical Association, and Barry Lewis, NSW Fire Commissioner and former Deputy Lord Mayor of Sydney.

The list of our opponents, the incumbent directors, read 'like a page from Who's Who', the *Sydney Morning Herald* reported in a lengthy article on the battle in October 1986. They included the Professor of Australian Literature at Sydney University and former ABC chairman, Dame Leonie Kramer, former CBC Bank general manager Mr Norm Winckle, former Sydney Stock Exchange chairman Mr Alistair Urquhart and the director of Coles Myer retail chain, Mr Ken Coles (the husband of then Ascham principal Rowena Danziger). The group was headed by Jim Millner, chairman of the chemist chain Washington Soul Pattinson. 'The directors' group likes, and aims to maintain, the way the NRMA is run,' the *Herald* reported.

I became embroiled in this Sydney power battle through Lady Braddon, the woman who had called me up on 2GB ten years earlier to help solve her land tax problem. After I took up her case, Lady Braddon befriended me and Tina, or perhaps it was the other way around: Lady Braddon was finding it hard to make ends meet; at one stage Tina and I were taking meals up to her each week; we became a de facto Meals on Wheels service for her. Out of gratitude, and without consulting me beforehand, she recommended me to David Parker. To be honest, I said yes because it was easier to say yes than no, and it sounded like an interesting idea at the time. I didn't know a lot about the campaign; it was more a case of donating my name to his cause.

The election attracted a lot of controversy, the *Sydney Morning Herald* reported.

> Allegations have included overpayment of directors' fees, premature opening of ballot boxes, encouragement of staff to campaign on behalf of the Millner team and an inefficient voting method which favours sitting directors.
>
> The campaigning began in earnest when Mr Parker approached the press with allegations that 12 past and present directors had received fees for work on a committee that allegedly had never met. He applied to the Supreme Court's equity division for the recovery of $240,000 in fees plus $350,000 in interest.

In the end, Parker's team lost and I breathed a sigh of relief. I was drowning under my existing commitments, and I needed that level of heat like a hole in the head.

TIME FOR A BREAK

In 1987, on the eve of the next elections (which had become four-yearly), I decided to stand down from Woollahra Council. Over the ten years as an alderman, I always tried to speak clearly and with commonsense. But I didn't always succeed, and when I left the staff presented me with a list of my more memorable verbal transgressions, and reactions I had prompted:

> 'There are many people in the municipality with a hip complaint.' (1980)
>
> 'There is a law – you cannot do it in the street!' (1982)
>
> 'If you take care of the pounds, the pennies look after themselves.' (1984)
>
> 'Council codes have gone by the board and through the window.' (1984)
>
> 'If it had not been for the Town Clerk supporting it, I would have thrown it out.' (1984)
>
> 'All the elderly, the widows, would come with their husbands [referring to the pathway down to Redleaf pool].' (1984 again: it was a very good year)
>
> 'Get stuffed, mate.' (1987, said by Ald. Paul Pearce to me, after which he was asked to withdraw the comment)

'I withdraw calling him mate.' (Ald. Pearce)
'I have been fighting this toilet window for ten years.' (1987)
'It looks as if the toilet window has won, Henri.' (1987, Ald. Pearce in reply)

The night I retired in September 1987, the *Wentworth Courier* recorded the farewell speeches faithfully:

> Ald. Henri Aram stood at the end of the meeting on Monday night and made a personal statement to the council. 'I would like to express my grateful appreciation for the loyal support of my constituents and the many friends made among them over the years.'
>
> Those who will miss Ald. Aram's smiling face will be able to see him on television as a regular contributor to a new series aimed at providing information to the four million Australians in the over 50s bracket. [The program on Channel 10 did not last very long.]
>
> Ald. David Joel said Aram was 'a character, a loner who fought on his own ... sometimes winning, sometimes losing, sometimes walking out'. He added that Ald. Aram's financial knowledge had also been a plus for the council.

I also paid tribute to my old sparring partner, Paul Pearce, 'who was the only person who had ever told [me] to get stuffed on the front page of the *Wentworth Courier*'.

When the paper's long-time council reporter, Kim O'Connor, asked me the secret behind my longevity, I told her: 'cold water (my daily swim) and hot women'. Of course, this quote never made its way into print.

Though it was in many ways a relief when I left council, I missed the involvement, the cut and thrust of trying to make life better for my community. When people enter public office, nobodies become instant somebodies – and I met lots of somebodies during my time there.

Would I advise someone to go into local government today? No way! It's such a drain on your personal life. Yet it was an overwhelmingly positive experience for me, so much so that I strongly considered going into State government. I made more friends than enemies on council, and was well respected when I left.

Over the ten years, there were several achievements of which I was proud. My victory in the minimum rating system stands out as a highlight. Following my court challenge to the council in 1976, I successfully lobbied the State government to amend the laws.

I also fought for years to have access through Double Bay Park to Redleaf Pool, on New South Head Road, because so many elderly people could not climb the steps. After many battles, I finally succeeded in persuading council to allow public access from the park adjoining the pool.

Another important victory was in relation to dogs in Nielsen Park. I love dogs but I don't like to swim with them. I have been a regular swimmer at Nielsen Park for many years, and dog owners thought it wasn't hurting anyone to bring their beloved pets into the water with them. I disagreed, for hygiene and safety reasons. I got council to eventually put up a notice – 'No dogs allowed on the beach'.

There was one man with a huge Labrador which he allowed to swim there. One day I stopped him as he came out of the water: 'Look, sir, there's a notice here – No dogs allowed on the beach. I'm a regular swimmer, and quite frankly I think you should follow the rules.'

'My dog doesn't go on the beach,' he said.

'But your dog is always in the water.'

'Yes, but I carry it across the beach to get there!'

I went back to council to have the sign amended, and didn't see him carrying the dog after that.

A PRIVATE LOSS

While the decade spent on council was rewarding professionally, my personal life was marred by loss and tragedy. My mother, who was an educated and intelligent woman, developed an irrational fear of stomach cancer. There was no reason for her to think like this. However, in her later years she refused to eat and virtually starved herself – despite being otherwise healthy for a woman in her seventies. At one point she had to have surgery to separate the walls of her stomach, which had grown together due to lack of eating. Towards the end she was so weak that she had to move to the Montefiore Nursing Home in Hunters Hill. She died in 1978, at the age of 83.

My mother's health and decline was, however, overshadowed by the problems faced by Tina at the same time. In 1973 she had an appendix operation, which revealed a slight potential abnormality in the tissue around her appendix. The surgeon suggested chemotherapy just to be sure. Tina resisted; she was against such debilitating treatment. Sadly, the surgeon's fear was justified when Tina developed intermittent bleeding in the cervix; she was diagnosed with cancer of the cervix – a condition her gynaecologist didn't recognise. Then she started chemo but it was too late.

For the latter half of the 1970s – while I was building up my own advisory business, appearing on radio, writing columns and standing on Woollahra Council – Tina's health went downhill. From 1980 onwards she suffered terribly as the cancer spread through her body. There were times when I thought I just could not carry on – the workload, caring for Tina, and our daughter Jackie, who was only ten when her mother entered the final phase of her illness.

In the lead-up to the 1983 local council elections, I wanted to step down to care for Tina and Jackie. Even though she was near the end, Tina insisted I stand again; it was almost a plea from her deathbed. She knew how much I enjoyed serving the community. In truth, I think I campaigned for that election for her, not myself. The elections were held in September 1983 and I was re-elected comfortably after a tough, drawn-out campaign. In a notice published by the *Wentworth Courier* in October, I wrote, among other thank yous:

> To my wife, whose moral support encouraged me to again join the 'bull-fight' of an election campaign.

One month later, Tina passed away, in November 1983, aged 48. The Mayor of Woollahra, Jock MacCallum, noted Tina's passing with a kind note in his weekly report:

> Mrs Aram was a most charming person who always went out of her way to help people in any way she could and she will be missed sadly by all who knew her.

My first book, *Money Matters,* was published just before Tina died. I remember the timing because at her funeral service at Darling Point one speaker mentioned that she lived just long enough to see its publication – the book was on her bedside table at St Vincent's Hospital. Living in the large Double Bay home, which had provision for live-in accommodation for nursing staff and a housekeeper, now became a burden. It was a low point in my life.

Tina's drawn-out illness and death, followed by three more years as an alderman, were hard enough but Woollahra Council pushed me over the edge when it proposed a rule demanding that aldermen declare their financial assets. I didn't object to that per se, provided they were assets that may be considered in conflict with council management or the municipality. By that I mean excluding assets such as shares or property elsewhere. My daughter Jackie was then eleven, and unbeknown to me these assets that I had earlier declared in good faith would now become available for public scrutiny. They were kept by the Town Clerk in a register, and under the Freedom of Information Act became available to the public at large.

That concerned me a great deal, not because I didn't want to disclose my assets. Rather, it was that they were now in the public domain. People would be able to work out the routines of your life, and be able to track your movements – when you went to work, when you were not at home ... and when my daughter was alone at home with a nanny. It made me feel vulnerable. I had been planning to stand in 1987 but changed my mind at the last minute due to this new policy. My seat was uncontested and a candidate from the Action Committee took over unopposed. I had heard stories about prominent businessmen and public figures, and their families, being exposed; I was not prepared to risk anything happening to my family at the time. Although my decision was held against me by some people, I couldn't have cared less. Unless you've been in the situation where you've lost your wife and were suddenly faced with being a single parent in a big house, you don't know what it's like. I wasn't prepared to be in the public spotlight under those circumstances.

A number of people raised eyebrows at what I did. 'You should have anointed somebody else, not dropped it,' they said. That is perhaps where I might have made an error of judgment. However, the loss of my wife made every decision much harder than it would have otherwise been. I have every sympathy with people under stress who do things they wouldn't normally do. Under the circumstances, I wonder if anyone would have acted differently. Anyone who knew the real reasons behind my decision saw the logic, from both a professional and personal perspective.

After Tina died, I fell apart. Her loss was the biggest shock of my life. From her death in 1983 until I resigned from council in 1987, I was a single father who had to go out on council committee inspections at all hours and take care of an eleven-year-old daughter in between work, council and newspaper commitments. They were the most difficult years of my life, and I don't know how I managed to keep going into work every day. In those days, my practice had an appointment every hour. I was booked out for weeks on end, hour by hour, but thanks to my capable secretary, Gloria O'Brien, was able to manage. In between, I had to do the newspaper columns and the radio. All-round, it was a terrible time. Trying to juggle my job, my daughter and running a household was a disaster; I fell into deep depression for a while.

Everywhere I looked, especially in the media, I was reminded of the pain of her passing. I could not stop myself from weighing into public debate over caring for the terminally ill, and wrote this letter to the *Herald* in February 1985:

> There is increasing concern in all major hospitals for the overall care for cancer patients. There are attached to these hospitals specialists in pain control who, together with their expert nursing staff, care humanely and compassionately for the dying. It would do them a grave injustice if this were not publicly acknowledged and would deprive those who may face death perhaps a little sooner than the rest of us of this vital reassurance.
>
> Where Australia is lagging is in the abysmal lack of cancer information, public education and back-up support for patients and their families.
>
> What is needed is for the Department of Heath, together with the State Cancer Council, to take a lead in developing institutional-based cancer-patient support groups, and in co-ordinating the numerous but now fragmented activities in all areas of cancer treatment and management.

The Cancer Council's Medical Director, Gordon Sarfaty, replied with a letter to the *Herald* shortly after.

> The NSW Cancer Council is aware of deficiencies in cancer management, education and support of cancer patients and their families, as expressed by Alderman Henri Aram, although we do not completely agree with his views on these matters.

Since then the Chris O'Brien Lifehouse at RPA has filled the void, determined to 'engineer a future without cancer'. It is now one of my favoured charities.

As if this wasn't hard enough for Jackie, at the age of thirteen she was diagnosed with Type 1 diabetes. Whether it was due to the shock of losing her mother, genetic disposition or just plain bad luck, I would never know. But this created an immense administrative problem because she had to have certain food at certain times. I had to begin a new way of living, starting with a housekeeper. I could write a book just on that subject alone. As a single father with a public profile, I attracted a certain type of applicant, and I went to my solicitor for advice. 'What protection do I have as a single person in a house alone with a woman housekeeper if she said that I'd gone to bed with her?'

'You have no protection,' he said.

This was a real worry, which was borne out by a housekeeper from New Zealand. One day Jackie said to me: 'You know she has wine in her room?' On top of that, when I came home at about six at night she would meet me with a towel around her, fresh from the shower. I had to get rid of her.

I then employed a Chinese girl who admitted she wasn't very good at cooking. But she had a partner, who could cook 'if I could accommodate him as well'. I didn't have many alternatives. Food and diet had become an absolute priority. They settled in well and for a while the house ran smoothly. Then I started getting enormous household bills. I went into their staff quarters and it was filled with bags of sugar and rice – not for a household of three people but for a large family of ten. In addition, they were running a business, importing sunglasses from Hong Kong.

Meanwhile, there were a few women of my milieu who saw me as target but for other reasons. I was a single father, with a daughter, 60 years old and in good health. Sonia McMahon, who we knew from Ascham school, took a shine to me. Tina and I saw the McMahons often, through school and social events. Sir William, the former Prime Minister, had asked for my advice in the 1970s shortly after his retirement from politics. He ran a business office in the Westfield building in William Street, and confided that he had been asked to support the launch of a property trust.

'Should I support it?' he asked.

'Sir William, personally I would not give my name to a property trust.'

I don't think he did, and the trust went bust. Sir William was later stricken with cancer and died in 1988, aged 80. Sonia was only 55 at the time and she continued to enjoy a prominent role in Sydney's social scene until she passed away in 2010.

Another renowned politician and diplomat, Sir Percy Spender, became our friend and confidant. Sir Percy had been our guest at the carp banquet in the 1970s and Lady Jean Spender became good friends with Tina through their involvement with the Black and White Committee. When Lady Spender died, Sir Percy often sought solace at our home, which at the time rumbled incessantly with the sound of excavation work being done for the Eastern Suburbs rail line at Edgecliff. Following one of Sir Percy's visits one night, we were awoken by a loud crash on the road. We dressed hurriedly and rushed across the road where we saw the tail-lights of a car that had careered into the excavation and the future rail line. By the time police and ambulance arrived we had managed to pull the driver and his companion from the wreckage.

It then fell to me to ring Sir Percy's son, John, to contact Paddington Police and bail out his brother Peter, the driver of the car, before his father found out what happened. Although he was somewhat inebriated, Peter Spender and his passenger escaped serious injury.

Some years later Sir Percy's then wife, the former Esme Esdaille, sought my advice as a client in relation to a family dispute. I had to decline because of a perceived conflict of interest. John Spender had meanwhile married fashion designer Carla Zampatti, who we both knew socially and through my council activities.

Around this time a little old lady with plastic bags walked into my office looking every bit like a bag lady, and asked my secretary to book a consultation. My secretary thought it strange and came into my office for advice. We concluded she must be a crank, I agreed to have a quick chat with her and asked her to send the woman in. My secretary had taken her name but somehow it did not register. The woman told me she had inherited a terrace house in Paddington, and as she already owned other property in Paddington someone had suggested she sell her inheritance and invest the proceeds in the stock market.

'Forget about the stock market,' I told her. 'You're better off renting out the new terrace. It will give you an income and will be easier to manage than a portfolio of shares. They need constant attention and I don't think that's what you want spend your time doing.'

She accepted that answer, thanked me politely and left. I didn't charge her for the advice. It was only a few weeks later, when my secretary was going through the records, that we realised why the name sounded familiar. I rang her recorded number. 'This is Margaret Olley,' her recorded message started.

When she returned my call, I asked her why she didn't tell me she was the famous artist.

'You never asked,' she replied drily.

'I would very much like to buy one of your paintings if you are so disposed.'

She thanked me and never gave me an answer, a source of mild regret when I heard the news of her death in 2011.

Just when I thought I would never find a decent housekeeper, I hit the jackpot: a Hungarian woman named Ilona who had worked for the

McMahons. As housekeeper jobs go, I thought that would have been a prize position. 'Why are you leaving them?' I asked politely.

'I had a falling out with Lady Sonia,' she explained.

'I won't hold that against you,' I replied.

I was lucky with Ilona because she was a mother who needed the money but wasn't looking for a husband; she had two daughters herself who lived in America. She was divorced from her husband and needed a job to support her daughters there. She was very efficient and friendly, though her personal hygiene was a problem. She had two dresses, one to wash and one to wear. The trouble was she never used the shower in the bathroom; she did all her personal washing in the laundry. It soon became a problem, at least for me. Jackie couldn't have cared less about the hygiene because they got on well together – which was the main thing. But I felt it was rather strange she was using the laundry instead of the shower, and was troubled by the odour that always followed her around. It was especially awkward at dinner time. But after all the trouble from previous hired help, this seemed a small price to pay. She stayed with us for a couple of years until I moved to a suitable unit in Edgecliff Road, nearer to Ascham school where Jackie was enrolled. In my youth in Berlin, Arnold and I mostly walked to school. I followed that principle with Jackie.

There were numerous other odd characters, including one woman who had so many visitors that I suspected she was running a brothel in the staff quarters of my Double Bay flat. When I confronted her over my suspicion, she told me she was a clairvoyant. 'Your future doesn't look stable,' she advised me, looking at my hand. 'And neither does yours,' I said, then gave her notice.

Next I saw an ad from a woman in Canberra, who had an Austrian name and background. She was looking for a job as a live-in. 'Come, and we'll talk about it,' I replied. She was a very big woman, loud and dominating, but the block of units was generously proportioned, including live-in quarters for the housekeeper, plus a bathroom. While I was thinking it over, she rang to say she had accepted a job in the nearby suburb of Vaucluse. Then, without warning, she returned a few weeks later, this time with her daughter, an attractive girl in her early twenties with a two-year-old child in tow. 'My daughter is looking for a live-in job and is happy to work for you,' she said. 'What about her child?' 'You'll manage,' she replied. I could see this was heading straight for the bedroom. I politely told her I was not an employment agency and bade her farewell.

Though my personal life was in turmoil, my appetite for speaking out against bad planning or regulations remained as keen as ever. One such problem was the aggression of bicycle couriers as they travelled around the Sydney CBD, which took me back to my youth when I was knocked off my own bike while riding into the city to work for David Jones. I wrote about this danger regularly to the newspapers, first to the *Australian* in May 1990.

> I express understandable concern at the ever-increasing dangers to pedestrians and road users generally at the proliferation, particularly, in the [Sydney] central business district, of courier cyclists.
>
> As a long-term measure, all bicycles should be registered, with their registration number clearly displayed on the cycle and contribute to the maintenance costs of roads and government services. They should carry third-party insurance the same as any other owner of a vehicle or property that poses a potential risk to third parties.
>
> If the Government is serious in its Let the User Pay principle, then there is no reason why any one commercial activity should be

excluded from bearing its rightful share of the cost compared with any other. To forestall the likely criticism from the leisure cycle lobby, registration costs could be restricted to third-party insurance premiums only.

Little was I to know that later the next year, in November 1991, I would get hit and knocked over by one of these same bicycle couriers in Martin Place, suffering a bad bruise on my buttock and leg. The first people to help me were staff from the nearby Commonwealth Bank, who took me into the bank and sat me down while I recovered. Coincidentally, they told me, one of the bank's senior managers recently had the same experience – being knocked over by a bicycle courier – and was off work, still in hospital, with a similar injury to mine.

I recovered quickly from the bruises and sent off a volley of correspondence, not just to the papers but to the Premier, and a formal submission to the NSW Liberal Government's Staysafe Committee, about getting couriers out of pedestrian zones. The Town Clerk of Sydney City Council replied:

> As you might be aware, Council has initiated a number plate identification scheme for bicycle couriers operating in the CBD, together with a Code of Conduct for such couriers. The scheme has been in operation for approximately 12 months and relies on the co-operation of the courier industry to monitor and regulate the activities of its couriers.
>
> Unfortunately, the scheme has not been fully successful in eliminating the hazardous and illegal riding of bicycle couriers. [I would never have known!]
>
> In regard to the problems encountered by yourself, Council has requested that the courier company, Allied Express Transport, take appropriate disciplinary action against the cyclist involved in the accident.

To the credit of then NSW Premier, Bob Carr, the matter was raised in State parliament, but like all the other undertakings – from the government, the Staysafe Committee and others – it came to the same conclusion: no change. At least I gave them something to think about. Twenty years on, nothing has changed.

The NSW government wasn't the only one making stupid decisions. The Federal Labor Government introduced legislation in the 1992–93 budget that would inflict an unfair punishment on pensioners. The effect of the legislation was that pensioners who had unrealised capital gains on shares would have those profits assessed against their pension entitlements. That is, if their shares appreciated in value, the increase over their purchase price at the end of the financial year would be considered a profit, even if the shares were not sold. If the price dropped the next day, the shares would still be deemed to have made a capital gain. It was ludicrous. I knew it and so did the public; letters poured in to my column at the *Australian* from nervous pensioners. This one (July 1993) summed up their anxiety perfectly:

> QUESTION
> I have just received a pamphlet from the Department of Social Security illustrating the (proposed) method of assessing share profits and losses. Upon evaluating my own situation, I am shocked by the result. With a portfolio covering only four different stocks and valued in total at less than $60,000, I stand to lose more than $130 a week, reducing my pension from its present $485 to only $210.

The amount shown as assessable is more than 50 per cent of imputed profits. As a pensioner, I cannot afford to play Russian roulette with my income. In any case, I would not willingly join in a game with the Government where they take 60 per cent of the profits and I suffer 100 per cent of the losses.

Would you still advise me to hang on to the shares, or have I made a mistake somewhere in my calculations?

ANSWER

Unfortunately, your calculations are correct. Widespread public concern at this incomprehensible piece of legislation has led the Senate to refer it to a standing committee on community affairs ... The outcome of this enquiry and the timing of repeal legislation, if at all, is unpredictable. Under the circumstances, and somewhat reluctantly but with time running out, it may be wise to turn your portfolio into cash before the September [23] deadline [for it to come into effect].

I decided to take up the challenge personally and made a submission to an enquiry convened by the Senate, setting out my concerns about the proposed legislation. The Senate Committee overseeing the matter invited me to appear before the enquiry. I was excited; I had never done this before but I was determined to bring the government to account and highlight the folly of their plan.

On the appointed day, I made my way down to Canberra, all alone, nervous but full of anticipation. After a short wait outside, where I saw a number of older people waiting in the hallways, I was ushered into an anteroom in Old Parliament House, where I stood before a broad bench of politicians. In the public gallery, a large crowd of pensioners had gathered to watch me argue on their behalf – although I had not spoken to anyone beforehand. Nor was I approached while in Sydney. Nevertheless, they clearly identified me as their advocate, and as I stepped up to answer the politicians' questions an air of expectation whizzed around the chamber. I was impressed by the number of pensioners who had made the trip down there.

The questions flowed quickly and I spoke for twenty minutes, off the cuff, though I had prepared my case in meticulous detail beforehand. I think the politicians were impressed, and I felt that I had convinced them that the proposed policy was a mistake because of the fundamental inequity. 'Unrealised capital gain can change every day,' I told them. 'Today's profit can be tomorrow's loss, and return to profit again the day after. How can that be assessed against a pension when it has not been liquidated?'

At the end of my statement, a round of applause and murmur of approval could be heard from the gallery, punctuated by some quick shouts of congratulation. 'Well done, Henri,' they said. I walked out, feeling that I had presented a strong case in support of my argument, and hoped that the pensioners would get some justice from my efforts. I was unprepared for what lay outside the big wooden doors: dozens of people were waiting and as I appeared they showered me with banknotes – both in congratulation but also as a measure of practical support to keep fighting the case. I declined the bank notes but I was overwhelmed. In all my years as a public advocate for commonsense and the interests of ordinary people, I had never felt so strongly the power of my words and ideas. I didn't know any of these people personally yet they made me feel I was one of them. In the weeks afterwards, back in Sydney, I continued to receive letters from worried, but increasingly desperate, people.

The government did not get back in touch with me again over my campaign. However, it ultimately decided to repeal the legislation. To what extent this was due to my action and advocacy, in print and in person, I do not know. I had to wait another six years or so to get my answer. In 1999 I received an Order of Australia, and the citation made specific mention of my appearance before the Senate Standing Committee.

STRANGERS ON A TRAIN

One of the bonuses of living close to Edgecliff station was that I could take the train into work each day. Every morning a regular group waited at the station and I developed a nodding relationship with others who I saw on the platform. Among them was an attractive Japanese woman who caught the same train as me. One day I saw that she was carrying a stack of financial prospectuses under her arm, and on the top was Australian Guarantee Corporation (AGC), which in those days was a highly regarded finance company.

Sitting next to me on the train, she started leafing through the various booklets. I plucked up the courage and said: 'Would you mind if I interfere, because I notice you have a stack of financial prospectuses for investment?'

She looked at me, puzzled. 'What do you mean?'

'I just thought I'd let you know that the AGC is the best one,' I explained.

When we met again she told me she was a secretary to the Consul-General for Japan, and he had given her strict advice about how to behave in Australia. 'Be very careful when you meet Australian men on the train, they're only after one thing,' he told her.

'My Consul said I must be very careful.'

'He's absolutely right,' I confirmed.

Her name was Kumiko. She was about 30; I was in my early sixties. One thing led to another, and during the late 1980s we became friends and developed a 'relationship'. Our friendship was shaped by the subtleties of Japanese manners and customs. When the Japanese say yes, it doesn't always mean yes. When I asked: 'Will you go out with me?' she said yes, which only means she would go out with me but not necessarily accept such an invitation at any given time.

Kumiko came from a wealthy Japanese family and was keen to settle in Sydney; she wanted to buy a unit. She had rented a unit in a small block on New South Head Road. I still owned Knowle, and managed to lease it to the Vietnamese Government, which took the whole house as a consulate. Jackie and I had meanwhile moved into a comfortable 1930s block called Cumberland on Edgecliff Road, near the corner of Ocean Street.

Kumiko and I became companions. After a decade or so of reshaping my private life following Tina's passing, especially ensuring that Jackie's life was stable, I enjoyed the company of an intelligent and attractive woman. We went to concerts and dinners, took a holiday to New Zealand together; she also came swimming with me at Nielsen Park at Vaucluse, a daily morning ritual I started when I was married to Tina . 'Henri's got an Asian bird,' the regulars would say as we walked along the beach. The sentiment wasn't malicious, or racist. Rather, it noted the disparity between our ages and my ability to attract a woman so much younger than myself. I certainly didn't take it the wrong way. I was happy.

My daughter Jackie did not respond as I had expected. I thought she would be upset by the age difference, or the fact that I was seeing someone relatively soon after her mother had passed away. Instead, she thought that if I could have a lady with me, she could have a boy. I didn't accept her logic, which created some friction between us.

'If my father can do it, why can't I?' she said

'I'm older than you,' I told her.

'That doesn't matter.'

It did but the negotiation was difficult, as she was around sixteen or seventeen at the time. We had a lot of arguments behind closed doors, loud enough for the neighbours in our apartment block to hear, even through thick double brick walls.

During our four years together, Kumiko introduced me to her brother and her family. We grew close and the age difference was not a problem for either of us. Kumiko wanted to get married; she wanted a child and thought I would be a good father for that child. Although I was fond of her, and felt flattered, I wasn't prepared to take the final step. The reasons are hard to articulate. Perhaps it was the combination of the age difference, and projecting forward to the burden of a young child when I was an older man, and the potential problems that might be involved with a child that is half-Japanese and half-Caucasian. (Edgecliff Station appeared to be a magnet for attractive Japanese women. Many years later another one, every much younger, caught my eye. But that is another story.)

The issue came to a head and we split up. Kumiko was disappointed but pragmatic. She found a Japanese man soon after, married him and had a child. Unfortunately, they got divorced but I remained friends with Kumiko, and advised her on investments over the years. She later became involved in the management of the Japanese cemetery in Cowra, the town in central western NSW where Japanese prisoners were interned during World War II and staged a mass breakout.

My reluctance to marry Kumiko was also based on what I knew from my brother Arnold, who had married a Japanese woman and raised two sons there with her. The problems for him were real and complex. The elder boy, named Anthony, came to Sydney to work for a leading accountancy firm, which had Mitsubishi among its clients. Anthony took a fancy to the secretary of Mitsubishi's chairman in Australia. Having been raised according to orthodox Japanese custom, he enquired from his boss if he could ask the secretary of the client company to go out with him for dinner. 'We have no objections, but I think if you're so concerned you should ask the director of Mitsubishi,' his boss told him. The head of Mitsubishi was wary. 'I am the guardian of this girl, and I'd have to put it to her father.' The father was biased against non-Japanese (Ganji). My nephew, being of half-Caucasian blood, was not a full Japanese. 'But if you think he's a reliable man, that's okay with me,' the father finally told Mitsubishi.

That was the start of their relationship and soon they became engaged. My brother rang me up with the good news: 'Anthony wants to bring out his fiancée to meet you.'

'I would love to meet her,' I told him enthusiastically. To my complete shock, his fiancée turned out to be the other Japanese lady I saw regularly on the Edgecliff train. Now I could give my blessing properly, as I had known her for some time and could attest to her, if nothing else.

When Anthony finally got engaged he felt the weight of family history and declared: 'I want to visit Oma's grave.' (Oma is the German word for grandmother.) It was a rainy day as together we left the cemetery. Anthony placed two photographs on the grave, where my mother's ashes were kept: one of himself and one of his future wife. Then he put a stone on them.

'Anthony, the photos will blow away, or get wet,' I told him.

'No, please, they must stay there,' he replied.

Arnold thought it was a strange thing to do but I didn't. Anthony was presumably appealing to my mother to intervene through the Almighty, and persuade the girl's parents to give their approval of the marriage. Although they were engaged, her parents had to approve the marriage because the children would be Ganji, and they thought that would make life more difficult for them than if she married a Japanese man. They were right.

For the younger son, Alexander, this problem may have been compounded by his marrying a Korean girl. The Japanese and the Koreans are not on the best of terms thanks to war and other historical issues. In spite of this, Alexander's mother, Yuki, generously welcomed her into the family.

Alexander, who I had met only briefly at my mother's eightieth birthday when he was about four years old, now works for Barclays Bank. During our recent trip, in 2010, he told me: 'We know nothing about our family. My father, during our early years, always travelled – in China, and Japan and Australia and Europe. He was never home.' My nephews were brought up virtually single-handedly by their mother, Yuki, who did an excellent job and who deserves great credit for her love and labour. I think Arnold regrets this now. It was difficult for the boys to accept that they were Ganjis. In reality they are more Japanese than the Japanese. But from the strictest racial point of view, they weren't accepted fully in Japan because they're half-European. And that has proved a handicap to the boys who, to their credit, have managed to overcome it.

Despite the recent earthquake and tsunami, Arnold is very happy

Arnold outside his Tokyo home, in 1990

in Japan, he doesn't have any longing to come back to Australia. My brother can live anywhere. If he has a room somewhere, he's happy. He's not so interested in personal accommodation and luxury. He has a modest home in Japan, and he built another one on the same site. Arnold stayed with Heine Brothers until Walter Heine died; the company wound down, and by mutual consent he was allowed to retire. By then he had developed other interests, especially share investing. In recent years, he has gradually lost some of his hearing and found satisfaction in following the stock market, which requires alertness and good sight, but not hearing. On the other hand, the loss of hearing has tended to imprison him; his sons have frequently told me they have felt as though they are losing their sense of family. 'He's now so deaf we can't get anything from him, and we know nothing about our family. Could you tell us?' Anthony asked. Hopefully, this book provides an answer.

ROBIN TAKES OVER

When I moved into T & G Building in the 1960s, a friend of mine asked me to join him one day at Nielsen Park in Vaucluse, which had picturesque harbour baths and kiosk nestled in among its leafy parkland. I had nothing better to do so I went along. It was a hot summer's day and I enjoyed myself immensely. It took me about an hour to get there and back, but when you enjoy something you find a way to fit it in. The experience was, in fact, a revelation. Physical activity was foreign to me as a child; my parents saw sport as a distraction from the higher pursuit of education. This chance invitation planted a seed within me. Soon I was swimming each day before I went to work and it became part of my routine. The attraction was not just physical. It was also enjoyable on a social level. I met quite a lot of people there – the Consul for Tunisia became a close friend. There were politicians and diplomats, judges and doctors. Abe Lander and his son, Paul, who became Attorney-General of NSW, were regulars.

An informal class system developed at Nielsen Park over the years. At the beginning, there were three groups of people who swam there. The Coolong Road mob, the old money establishment set who were named after the nearby wealthy street, swam at the top next to the showers. Next was the consular corps (the Arabs and Middle-Eastern diplomats), and then there were the Jews, nicknamed the Knesset (the name for the Israeli Parliament). The Knesset mob had a theme song, 'Onward Christian Soldiers', foisted upon them by the others. They in turn would whistle it whenever the Coolong Road mob went by. In the early years, Tina occasionally tried to bring the various factions together with a champagne breakfast at Christmas or New Year's Day. Although the idea never caught on permanently, all three groups enjoyed swimming next to each other over the years. It did, however, prove that with the right amount of goodwill, people can come together, and leave political or racial differences behind them.

In the 1990s, one of the regular swimmers, a lady from the Coolong Road mob, approached me one day as I got out of the water. Her husband read my newspaper column and had written to me for advice about his business problems. He had been treated badly by a leading bank and his predicament was affecting not only his business but his marriage and livelihood. I was aware of his letter and situation but was unable to help as it involved legal matters that only a solicitor could resolve. The couple eventually divorced, and following our initial contact we started waving at each other as we followed our own early morning swim routines.

At the time I was in a friendly social relationship with a widow whose late husband had headed a thriving construction company that later got into difficulties as a result of unexpected competition. He had earlier sought my financial advice and we became friends and mixed socially; I maintained the friendship with his widow after he died. She was well connected and her husband had built a block of units right on the harbour foreshore in a gorgeous position, which offered the opportunity of lavish parties, particularly with major sailing events such as the annual Sydney–Hobart yacht race on Boxing Day, when a Who's Who of the Sydney social scene, and the professions, were invited guests.

Through this milieu I was introduced to members of the Royal Motor Yacht Club in Point Piper and ended up being elected to the board – even though I didn't own a yacht! To my surprise, the RMYC's secretary turned out to be none other than the charming lady from the Coolong Road mob at Nielsen Park (who had introduced herself as Robin) and was now divorced. After the board meetings I would occasionally drive her home to her house in Woollahra, which was also on my way home. While I always maintain she was the mermaid who chased me, Robin insists to this day that it was the opposite – that I chased her! Although nearly twenty years younger than me and the mother of two active teenagers, neither of these factors seemed to matter.

We started going out in 1992 and became closer and closer, so much so that eventually Robin was able to arrange for me to be invited to join the swimmers at the Coolong Road mob and enclave at the showers.

Over the next few years my relationship with Robin blossomed while my earlier companion, the widow, stayed in the picture. While we never had any romantic attachment and our arrangement was purely social, it appeared she still had her own ideas, and possibly designs on me. When I moved to Overthorpe in 1993, Robin offered to come and help me. The widow was confined to her home with a bad flu but halfway through the move, as the furniture arrived at the unit, she rang to see how I was going. She did not know about my relationship with Robin.

'Hello! Who's that?' she asked when Robin picked up the phone.

Robin replied: 'Who's that?'

That ended my friendship with the other lady, and with it the annual Sydney–Hobart yachting festivities!

Robin grew up in a loving home environment. Her parents had owned a small terrace in Woollahra and were reasonably comfortable. Her husband had built a graphics business, and when this faltered had earlier sought my advice through my column in the *Sydney Morning Herald*. He was commodore of the Prince Edward Yacht Club, where he moored their yacht and navigated under Robin's command. But in business they had trouble getting paid on time and became overcommitted, to the extent that her parents' small terrace had been pledged to the Australia Bank as security for a business loan made under very tough conditions.

During the 1987 crash the business went broke. It affected the family: her marriage broke up because of their financial problems, and both her sons Jason and Marcus were moved from an expensive private school, Cranbrook, just before doing their HSC. At the time, Robin faced a battle to keep their education going. But her persistence and sacrifice paid strong dividends. Both have become successful in their fields. Jason is a partner in an animation business, exporting internet games. Marcus works for the government in Canberra, the manager of a team that supervises the coordination of national criminal checks for organisations in Australia. Marcus has three children and Jason has four. I enjoy a cordial and close relationship with both boys and their expanded families. Jason, apart from his business acumen, is a successful stock market investor and currency trader. Marcus is more of a company man and expert in his field. To their credit they each are prepared to accept the occasional recitations of the life experiences of the old (stepfather) bloke.

When I heard that Robin's family home was being subject to a forced auction, I thought I could help by buying it and let them stay there. I went to the auction, and I was two minutes too late. In the 1980s I had tried, and succeeded, in a similar plan for an elderly lady who lived in my block of apartments in Edgecliff. The woman was living alone and her sister, and family, owned the apartment. When they needed the money, I struck a deal with her family to buy the unit from them and let their elderly aunt stay there for a nominal rent. I have always got a kick out of helping others in trouble. But with Robin, I was too late. So when I first took her out, she lived in a slightly cramped unit opposite the Russian Consulate in Fullerton Street, Woollahra.

Robin and me at our wedding, in 1999.

Robin's two sons Jason (left) and Marcus (right) at the wedding reception in the Ritz-Carlton, Double Bay

Des Eady, my best man, and his wife Joy

. Robin with her two sons and my daughter Jackie

In 1999, my life was marked by two memorable events. Firstly, I received an Order of Australia (OAM) in the Australia Day honours list. The citation started: 'For service to the community and to improving public awareness and understanding of the principles of finance and investment.' While I was touched by the letters of congratulations from politicians, bankers, friends and acquaintances, what really stood out in my mind was the second half of the citation: 'Mr Aram appeared before the Senate Standing Committee on behalf of pensioners holding shares in relation to the unrealised gains provisions. These were later repealed in the subsequent Federal Budget.' Here, among all the people I had advised and helped, was recognition that I had made a difference, a difference for the better.

The *Sydney Morning Herald* interviewed me and prepared an article (that was never published) but which the reporter forwarded on to me out of courtesy. Looking back, I seemed to enjoy going against the prevailing wisdom of the time:

> Henri Aram feels there ... is too much attention to 'gloom and doom' merchants and not enough hard thinking.
>
> 'People think if they invest in real estate they can't lose. They can. They can lose more money in that than anything else. It is ignorance that keeps people out of things where they can benefit. This negative gearing – if you are not paying tax, you are paying interest – it is being misrepresented.
>
> 'I have put pensioners into the Commonwealth Bank and National Bank and they have more money than they have [ever had] in their lives now. If the bank pays you three per cent on deposit and six per cent fully franked, why not buy some of their shares?'

The second highlight of 1999 was that Robin and I got married. I proposed to her three months beforehand, during a weekend at the Fairmont Hotel in Leura in the Blue Mountains, and we were married in the Carlton-Ritz Hotel at Double Bay. It was only a small wedding, a civil service with a celebrant (Robin is not Jewish. I always joked to her: 'If your mother had been alive, she'd have talked you out of marrying an old Jew'). This was followed two months later with a large reception in the same venue. The guests at our ceremony consisted of two of her friends and two of my best friends. My best man was Des Eady, the real estate agent friend who had helped me all through my life. Robin's sons and their wives attended, as did her best friend Adrienne, Maddy and her husband John, my daughter Jackie, and Tina's niece Karin from Germany.

Jackie has made her own way in life. It's not the life I expected her to lead. But you can't control your children's lives. She now lives in Blackheath, in the Blue Mountains west of Sydney, with her husband, Ian. They got married six years ago and now have a little daughter, Evelyn Christine. They live modestly; they like it that way. I don't really have much contact with her these days, and I wish we could see more of each other. There are forces in some lives beyond a father's love and in the end everyone must choose their own path.

Of the stack of letters I received following my OAM a few months earlier, I was touched by two simple notes from her:

> Dear Dad,
> After so many years of hard work and generosity to everyone, you deserve the award. Lots of love
> From your daughter, Jackie.

Then a few days later, a second letter.

Dear Dad,
I just want to congratulate you again on getting the order of Australia and of finally proposing to Robin. I want you to know too that I am very proud of you, proud to be your daughter and that ... I still love you very much. I miss you Dad. I wish things could be different between us ...

In the meantime, I must say it's so wonderful to hear you so happy!

From your daughter, Jackie

With the NSW Governor, Gordon Samuels, at the ceremony for my Order of Australia in 1999

(Right) With Robin in 1998 at Witzlebenplatz 5, the place of my birth

(Below) The Grunewald Villa in Treplitzerstrasse 7, Berlin, where we lived after our return from Paris in 1935

After our wedding Robin and I took an extended honeymoon to Europe. We flew first to London, took a cruise from Dover to Venice, and from there went on to Lake Como, then Germany and Switzerland. We loved travelling overseas, including a memorable trip in 1996 to the ruins at Petra in Jordan. During a tour of the Wadi, our guide said his uncle was a sheik and that he was looking for a third wife. To help him fulfil his conjugal obligations, the uncle always drank a lot of camel milk, which he claimed made him more virile, our guide told us.

'My uncle would give you three camels for your wife,' he told me after this explanation.

'I'm sorry. I won't take less than four,' I replied.

Robin giggled, the guide threw up his hands (apparently the price was too high!) and we moved on to the next bit of scenery.

During the trip we also visited Germany, where we went to a dinner with a family who lived in the same area. Our host was the retired head of the German Milk Board. 'Well, of course, we didn't all know what went on under the Nazis,' he said to me. His wife was refreshingly candid: 'Come on, we were all in it, you know as well as I do.'

'I appreciate your honesty,' I told her.

The funny thing is that when you go to Germany today, everyone seems to have a Jewish ancestor. There's a lot I admire about Germans and a lot I detest. Deep down, they were gutless. When they became aware of what was going on, they couldn't change it. Even the children were indoctrinated in school that if your parents say anything against the regime you must tell your teacher, and people in their own homes weren't safe anymore. They would be denounced and sent to work in labour camps, even if not sent to Auschwitz or the other death camps. I have been back there about half a dozen times, and my mixed feelings remain.

During my earlier years, Tina helped to advance my professional success and survival. When Robin came into my life, she actively promoted my physical survival. A health fanatic and true believer, rightly or wrongly, in every vitamin supplement promoted on the market, she is praised by all our friends for having contributed to my physical wellbeing. She has been responsible for prolonging my life expectancy and quality of life. For this I am grateful to her.

Now happily married, I continued to work at A.R.A.M. Investments through my eighties, my mind and interest in business as keen as ever. My body, however, has faltered occasionally. In 2004 I was diagnosed with bowel cancer. Robin likes to remind me that it coincided with our fifth wedding anniversary. I was admitted to St Vincent's Hospital in Darlinghurst, and Robin stayed with me until about 9.30 pm, when she reluctantly left me to spend the evening at home alone, the night before our anniversary. As she pulled off the doona to get into bed, Robin saw a box on the sheets, with a gold necklace and pearl-and-diamond drop, plus a card – of course.

Robin rushed in the next morning, before I went down to the operating theatre, threw her arms around me and covered me in kisses, thrilled at my little surprise. The operation was a success, the doctors cut out all the cancer and I didn't need any chemotherapy either. But nature had another go at me: a few years later the doctors told me I had cancer of the bladder. I beat that too, with the support of Robin and my new extended family.

Although Robin and I moved from the apartment in Edgecliff Road down the hill to a block called Overthorpe, on New South Head Road in Double Bay, I still owned Knowle. In 2003 it brought me fresh trouble when I applied to build four two-bedroom units in the garden fronting my property. My intention was largely to allow lift access to the residence at the upper level, which up to that time was accessible only by steep stairs and through the adjoining block of units, Colebrook, which had caused ongoing disputes for several years.

Woollahra Council, seeing the heritage report in my development application, decided to place a heritage listing on the whole property. I wasn't happy, and appealed to the Land and Environment Court, which ruled that the front garden could be excluded from the heritage order. But the council placed such conditions on permission for development that I couldn't go ahead with it. It was a case of déjà vu, as this property was the reason I got into local government in the first place. Two years later I finally sold Knowle to the Vietnamese Government, which had leased the property for several years as its consulate. 'Good riddance,' I said to myself. The court battle against exclusion of the front garden proved to be a battle worth winning; it enabled the Vietnamese Consulate to install an inclinator from the garage to the house years later to improve access across land that would otherwise have been heritage-listed and unusable.

UNFINISHED BUSINESS

I have never forgotten the debt of gratitude that my family owed Onkel Mor. When the Wall came down in Berlin in 1989, I said to Arnold: 'I think we should go to Germany.' I made enquiries to see if we could find Onkel Mor's grave. We eventually located it through a long-time friend of mine, who discovered that his ashes had been taken to a cemetery by his former secretary, Fraulein Gumpert. She deposited his ashes and signed in the registry that she was the only witness to the interment.

Onkel Mor committed suicide, so we still couldn't work out what sort of funeral he had. First of all, there must have been an arrangement with both Hedwig our housekeeper, and also Fraulein Gumpert, who was with him for ten to fifteen years. She had a club foot and there was no attachment between them, but she must have risked her life to help him, and probably assisted in the suicide. He was on heart tablets, and it appears he took an overdose to enable him to end his misery. They obviously kept it very secret because she faced a life sentence if she associated with a Jew or helped one, or worse still, collected his ashes for the funeral.

The search for the grave was a rather sad story. I wrote to the Jewish Gemeinde (the community organisation) in Berlin, asking if Onkel Mor was buried in their cemetery.

They replied that he wasn't there. But what I didn't know, nor did they tell me, was that Berlin had two cemeteries for Jews. One is where the Orthodox Jews are buried; the other one, Weissensee, allowed liberal and other Jews to be buried there. It must have been a liberal cemetery to accept ashes in the first place. So then another friend of mine, who lives in Frankfurt, went and searched the records at Weissensee – and that's where Mor's ashes were found.

When we found the grave, I suggested to Arnold that we set a memorial stone there, and also commemorate those Germans who had assisted Jews. I wrote to the Jewish Gemeinde again: 'We have found his grave and have invited the Mayor of Weissensee to attend.' The Gemeinde would not agree to send a representative to the ceremony. I requested that they send a rabbi, or member of the clergy, to say Kaddish, the traditional Jewish prayer for the departed. They refused on the grounds that Jewish law did not acknowledge cremation as a legitimate burial, and 'they could not honour a deceased with Kaddish where ashes are involved'. I was furious with them. There are six million Jews turned to ashes at Auschwitz, Treblinka and other camps who we mourn and honour year in year out. Yet they would not honour someone whose remains were cremated under different and desperate circumstances. It didn't make sense to me, and still doesn't.

In the European summer of 1998, the whole family came to Berlin. My brother and his wife from Japan; I went with Robin. My friend who found the grave came along, so did my friend from Israel, Fred Nomburg (now Yair Noam of Tel Aviv), who lost his entire family in Auschwitz at the hands of the Nazis. We shared the same school bench on our first day of school and have remained friends for over 80 years. I had only seen Fred four times in 60 years but kept in touch via hundreds of letters. Fred was the friend who initially expressed scepticism about me marrying Tina, a German, but was won over when he and his wife Anita met her.

The other person who attended was Karin, my German niece through Tina. It was a moving ceremony, a moment where all the points of my life came together. My parents would have loved to know that we did this. It's a shame they weren't around to be there.

The *Sydney Morning Herald* had a correspondent in Berlin at the time, Geoff Kitney, who I invited to the ceremony. The office of the Mayor of Berlin asked me to invite the heads of Schultheiss; the company sent its chairman as a mark of respect and regret for what happened to Onkel Mor. Fate takes funny turns. Schultheiss now have their main office right across the road from the burial plot in Weissensee where Onkel Mor is buried.

Kitney attended the ceremony and wrote a fine article about it:

> For Henri Aram, a Sydney financial adviser, the ceremony was the fulfilment of a long-cherished wish to acknowledge the part his uncle, Moritz Sachs, played in allowing him to escape from Germany and start a new life in Australia.
>
> 'Uncle Mor saved our lives, there is no doubt about that,' Mr Aram said. 'With his last savings he helped to raise the 30,000 marks which was demanded by the German government to procure the equivalent of $200 for the fares so our family could escape to Australia.
>
> 'For me, this is the completion of a journey … a happy, sad day.'
>
> For Mr Aram, now 75, the visit to Berlin was difficult because of the memories of what happened here to his family and friends during the Nazi persecution of the Jews.

'I wanted this to be a ceremony of reconciliation, and I am very pleased that is what it was,' Mr Aram said.

The memorial plaque mentioned three families: Riesenfeld and Rosenthal – both on my mother's side – and Nomburg, the family of my friend Manfred. Onkel Mor had nothing to do with the Nomburgs and my brother was bewildered at their inclusion in what was a very family matter. I included the Nomburgs out of respect to my friend, whose family had no other physical memorial of their history, anywhere. With Fred's family wiped out at Auschwitz, I wanted him to have some place he could go to visit in their memory.

He responded with a moving address at the ceremony:

> It is thanks to my parents' foresight that I am able to stand here today, it is thanks to the friendship of Henri that their name was honoured at long last here in Weissensee cemetery, where also my grandparents are buried.
>
> Sixty years ago my parents made all efforts to send me away to Palestine, while they themselves were denied a place of refuge, and were deported in 1941 along with many more Berlin Jews to a Polish ghetto and later to a death camp.
>
> Henri knew them well and as our friendship continued throughout all these years, decided to have my parents' name inscribed on the memorial dedicated to his and his brother's uncle, Mor.
>
> By doing so, my dear friend, you have added still another bond of friendship. You have my heartfelt thanks, also in the name of my entire family.

Although I was indeed satisfied with the ceremony, I was very unhappy with the behaviour of the Berlin Jewish Gemeinde. In the absence of clergy, Yair Noam recited the Kaddish.

There was a further bitter irony in this Schultheiss story. The chairman of Schultheiss presented me with a centenary book the company had recently published. The book showed that all the Jewish directors left the company in 1931, which was the time that this so-called fraud was discovered by the secretary of state. I pointed out to the Chairman that this was wrong. I had a letter of recommendation for my grandfather when he was forced to retire in 1933, and he had been there for 40 years. The Chairman admitted that this was an oversight and that it would be corrected in the next edition. They say history is written by the winners but I don't think there were any winners after what the Nazis did in and before World War II.

Onkel Mor's memorial at the dedication ceremony in 1998.

The headstone of Onkel Mor's memorial.

Arnold and Yuki paying their respects

Flowers of remembrance from the current management of Schultheiss brewery, where Onkel Mor was a director

And one from the Mayor of Berlin

My old school friend Manfred Nomburg (now Yair Noam), who flew from Tel Aviv for the ceremony. Left, a cartoon he drew for me when I joined Hestia in 1965.

With Manfred at the Witzleben-Leitzensee school in Berlin where we shared a school bench on our first day

Arnold and me at the memorial ceremony

Aram family possessions that were donated to the Jewish Museum of Berlin

Robin and me at the memorial dinner for Onkel Mor

Arnold and Yuki at the dinner

Tina's niece Karin with a government official who attended the dinner

I have remained acutely sensitive to the scales of justice in matters relating to Germany and the Jews. When the Danish prince Frederik married Australia's Mary Donaldson in 2004, I wanted to recognise the efforts of his grandfather (and namesake) during World War II, when he showed public resistance to the Nazis by riding his horse through the capital every day, and also slighting Hitler with a brief telegram in response to a letter of birthday congratulations. I wrote to the Danish Palace to tell them I wanted to make a donation to the Prince's favourite charity. 'Perhaps you would be kind enough to let me know how this best be achieved.' Two weeks later, the Palace replied that they had chosen the Crown Prince Frederik Fund for my donation. 'The fund was established in 1993 to commemorate Crown Prince Frederik's 25th birthday and his studies at Harvard University. Each year the fund offers two outstanding Danish students the opportunity to attend the Kennedy School of Government at Harvard.' The mention of Harvard was bittersweet; it reminded me of my own ambition to study there all those years ago.

Another such moment occurred in 2008, when the German Chancellor, Angela Merkel, made a speech before the Israeli Parliament, the Knesset, which touched a chord in me for its acknowledgement of Germany's legacy and responsibility. I decided to write to Mrs Merkel to thank her and ask to meet her on an upcoming visit to Berlin. Her office sent a letter of thanks. 'The sad fate of your family was noted with great compassion. The Bundes Chancellor was particularly pleased, therefore, about your gracious reference and appreciation of her speech.' Predictably, she was unable to find time to meet me, though I took satisfaction in the effort she made to reply.

The *Sydney Morning Herald* article about our memorial to Onkel Mor generated a heart-warming spinoff. Late in June 1998, barely a couple of weeks after the ceremony, I received a letter from a Dan Montague, who lives at Sorrento on the Mornington Peninsula in Victoria:

> Once in a while I buy a Sydney Morning Herald – I did last Saturday and read the moving story of your return with your brother to Berlin. How well it was written, with detail, not some six-line thing as is often the case.
>
> About five years ago I made an appointment to seek financial advice from you. In the course of our discussion and because he was my family, I mentioned the young Korean lad who was homeless and who I had taken under my wing. When it came time to go, you did not charge any fee but said: 'you have been charitable to the boy and I will be charitable to you.' I have never forgotten that, or you. The generous spirit of your uncle Mor runs through the family.
>
> I am glad you had the satisfaction of seeing to your uncle's memorial – a terrible sad task but you never gave up. You are a good and kind man and much more to want it to be also a reconciliation. What a lesson for us all.
>
> In closing, I want to tell you that the lad and I have persevered: it is now eight years, many ups and downs but I am happy to say he is a taxi driver in Melbourne, working full-time. He comes home regularly – home – yes, I did manage to buy a modest little house and pay for it outright – with a quarter acre of land.
>
> I will photocopy the article and keep it for Mickey (for that is what he changed his name to) so he will also not forget you.
>
> Yours sincerely,
>
> Dan Montague

ALAS, SIR WARWICK

The other unfinished business of the past decade related to my acquaintance with the Fairfax family (I have been on Lady Mary's Christmas card list for a number of years), which culminated in a mysterious episode that still puzzles me. In 2003 I had a client named Jean Walker, a pensioner, who wanted me to advise her on how to make extra money outside her pension. During our discussion about her financial situation, she told me her husband was a well-known war artist, Ralph Trafford Walker, who designed the doors of the New South Wales State Library in Macquarie Street, among other artworks. She said she was a sculptor, too, and took out some photographs to prove it.

With the experience of Tina's bust in the back of my mind, I suggested that she use her sculpting skills to make some extra money. 'I'll tell you what I'll do,' I said. 'I know the Fairfaxes. I will commission you to make a bust of Sir Warwick [whohad died in 1987], and then we can present it to Lady Mary.'

Mrs Walker liked the idea; so did Lady Mary who helped us find some photos of her late husband from the Fairfax family archives. Mrs Walker took my photos and fashioned an impressive bust. The news spread quickly. 'The local member came through the house to visit my husband, and he saw the bust of Sir Warwick,' she rang to tell me.

'How come you have a bust of Sir Warwick?' the local member asked.

'Henri Aram commissioned it.'

'That's fabulous. I'll get young Warwick [Mary's son] to view it,' the local member replied.

Sure enough, young Warwick was taken to the studio to see the bust of his father. Mrs Walker rang me up to report back. Warwick had told her she should adjust the mouth of Sir Warwick because he had never seen his father smile. 'That's not a problem. I'll fix it,' she told him. Mrs Walker had previously asked me for a photo that featured the back of Sir Warwick's head so she could finish it off, as all the other photos were frontal or side-on. Lady Mary then provided a suitable photo, which I sent on to Mrs Walker. Shortly afterwards, I had to go into hospital for a bowel cancer operation, and I had other things to think about instead of the bust after my recuperation. I clean forgot about the bust until a few years ago while cleaning my office files, when I came across the photographs Mrs Walker sent me of the sculpture.

I wrote to Lady Mary in July 2009, and sent the photos to her:

> My dear Lady Mary,
>
> While clearing out old records of my files in the city, we came across the attached photographs of a bust of Sir Warwick which, you may recall, I had commissioned from one of my old clients – a pensioner with what we perceived as artistic talents! This was shortly after Sir Warwick's passing and for which you provided the necessary photographs to enable the sculpture to proceed.
>
> What happened to the finished article I do not know but it was to be presented to young Warwick by the then member for the Northern Beaches – his name escapes me. It was my understanding your son sought some minor adjustments but whether they were

> completed I do not know. In any case I thought it a pity to discard and throw away this memorabilia in case it may of interest to you or members of your family.

J.B. Fairfax replied two weeks later, in August 2009.

> I have been in touch with Warwick Fairfax and he says that my reference to the bust of Sir Warwick is the first he has heard of it. He would, however, like the photographs and I shall forward them on to him. In the meantime he is going to check with his mother and her office as to whether they have any knowledge of what in my view is an extremely good likeness of Sir Warwick.

Nearly a year later, in June 2010, Lady Mary's personal assistant wrote to me:

> Unfortunately I have come to a dead end. I have spoken to several members of the Fairfax family as well as several other leads I had on the sculptor, with no success. Thank you once again for the photos. Should we eventually locate the sculpture, I will certainly let you know.

I have retained some of the photos of the bust but Lady Mary has the others. We tried to track down the Walkers through the State Library. Last I heard they were in a nursing home in Queensland somewhere. I don't know if they're still alive. Mr Walker never exhibited his art; he kept it all at home. I visited the Walkers a number of times. They had two studios and in hers the photos of Sir Warwick were strewn around. The bust itself was probably sold in a garage sale somewhere. On the other hand, it was never cast in bronze, only in plaster. So maybe it crumbled.

However, Mrs Walker later made me a bust of myself, as thanks for the help I had given her. It's very good. If only I could find the bust of Warwick. They would make a nice pair.

The bust of Sir Warwick Fairfax, by Jean Walker

A bust of me, also by Jean Walker

TURNING FULL CIRCLE

Sometime in 2005 my niece Karin in Germany alerted me to the establishment in Berlin of the Leo Baeck Institute as part of the Jewish Museum for the purpose of building up a collection of memorabilia and heritage items salvaged from the belongings of Berlin Jews who either had fled the country during the Nazi regime or were murdered in concentration camps during the war years and before.

The institute originated from donations in the USA and was named in honour of the famed Chief Rabbi of Germany during the 1930s who, in his own words 'would not leave Germany while a single Jew remained on German soil'. As I remembered his dedication to German Jewry well, the institute attracted my interest and support.

I contacted the head of the archives, a Canadian by birth named Aubrey Pomerance, who had settled in Berlin, and within a few weeks we had formed a friendly relationship. Eventually I donated my parents' cherished family records and the few treasures they had been able to retain from our hasty flight on Kristallnacht. The Abraham (Aram) collection was inaugurated with old family china, three commemorative birthday cups owned by my father (130 years old), my brother and myself. Over the years we found other objects, including my father's war records and my uncle's Iron Cross for bravery, awarded for an injury to his skull sustained while serving in World War I.

As my immediate family would have little ongoing interest and my brother's family was spread around the world or in Tokyo, it was agreed that the Berlin Museum would be the best guardian of the family's small heirlooms.

Aubrey Pomerance invited Robin and me for a visit and an educational lecture series for schoolchildren who were largely ignorant or poorly advised on the pain and suffering their parents and grandparents had inflicted on their fellow citizens for no other reason than that they happened to be of the Jewish faith. We made a couple of visits, the last in 2008 which we also combined with the Bar Mitzvah of Aubrey's son. Held in one of the halls of the building adjoining the former Oranienbuger Strasse famed old synagogue, the ceremony was conducted by a German woman who had converted to Judaism after the war and qualified as a rabbi.

In May 2008 the Leo Baeck Institute invited me to address a two-day workshop of schoolchildren from two different schools who had been given the chance to learn more about their country's recent and disturbing history. The first morning consisted of children from a public school, of both sexes, who were interested and polite and asked a lot of intelligent questions. They asked me how my family managed to live comparatively unscathed during the lead-up to the war: Neither your father nor Onkel Mor were ever arrested or put in a concentration camp, one student said. It was an unexpected question and I spent some time pondering why. I finally came up with the combination of factors that I hoped would explain it. My parents' reserved conduct and low profile played their part but perhaps the main reason was that we shared our home in the suburb of Grunewald with an SA General whose staff car had guarded the property day and night, unaware that it also housed two Jewish families who he was apparently willing to tolerate and live with. He showed no name plate on his door for possible identification, for reasons best known to him.

On the question of war service I surprised the children with the fact that my father was a Volunteer Front Soldat during World War I and that his cousin's husband had been awarded the Iron Cross for bravery in action, awarded to a Jew by none other than the new Commander-in-Chief of the armed forces, Adolf Hitler. They were astounded and could not understand why he should have had to flee to escape the gas chambers.

They asked about schooling and I explained that as Jews we were barred from sharing our education with non-Jewish schoolmates but had to go to either a foreign school (like the American School I attended) or a specific Jewish school like the one we attended before fleeing the country.

When they asked about the pogroms, I told them how all the windows on the Kürfurstendamm were smashed by Nazi hooligans and how the remaining Jewish community was denied insurance which was collected by the authorities. In addition, they had money confiscated specifically to pay for the damage inflicted on Kristallnacht, including a fine on our furniture packed for shipment to Australia. Some of the children responded with disbelief.

On emigration, I told them of the importance my parents attached to learning foreign languages instead of playing sport, with a view to starting life in some distant country, which proved a sound decision.

The second group the next day, also of both sexes, were friendly and congenial but came from a lower class public school. There were five troublemakers among them whose faces showed disrespect and little interest, if any, in my talk. In my discussions with their teacher afterwards, I was told that all that his students cared about was how they would spend their first day after they had the freedom of not having to go to school. The future held no interest for them and foreign languages least of all. This attitude pretty well summed up the German mentality and helped explain how the Nazis gained their foothold on an uneducated public.

We concluded our journey by joining my German niece Karin and her husband on a trip to Austria, where they travelled extensively and knew all the right places and best hotels. They had booked a couple of rooms at the famous Altaussee and its fashionable hotel, which bears the proud inscription 'Family owned for 150 years'. This is not unusual in Austria, where such phrases are supposed to convey some reassurance of the hotel's quality and service.

I always had a funny feeling in Austria. Every hotel you go to will pride itself on the fact that it was in 'family ownership for 150 years'. If the family has owned it that long, and they still own it, they must have been Nazis. Otherwise the government would have closed it down, cashiered your business. And every one of those establishments would have had a notice on it: 'Jews and Dogs are not allowed.' I go into these hotels and feel very, very uncomfortable because I know that I would not have been allowed in by that same family during my earlier, formative years.

Outside one hotel, they had a large lake for swimming, with a sign saying: 'Dogs not allowed.' I said to Robin: 'In my youth that sign would have read: "Juden und Hunden Verboten."'

As a boy we went with my father on a bike tour, and we couldn't stay anywhere overnight because Jews weren't allowed. So these days when I travel there I look for new hotels, nothing with a notice about being owned by the same family for 150 years. The internal conflict never goes away; you just learn to live with it. Of course, one of the problems in Germany was that Jews were very prominent. They worked hard, and had the brains to build up these businesses, in newspapers, in printing, in retail, in manufacturing. That was the problem: they were too prominent and smart for their own good.

It was only three years ago, during another visit to Germany, that we were invited to a stately Bavarian mansion stacked with the most exquisite Chinese art collection worth millions. The Bavarian host had married a Chinese lady who as well-connected with the current regime. During dinner he advanced the theory that both Hitler and Mao had done much for their respective peoples. This depends very much on which side of the fence you sit.

With Robin and the Governor-General, Major-General Michael Jeffery

The Aram-Stokes family at a reunion in Sydney to celebrate my eighty-eighth birthday in 2011

Another reunion, this time in Tokyo, on Arnold's ninetieth birthday

With Robin and Jackie at Anthony's wedding in Sydney

A dinner party in 2011 to celebrate Arnold's ninetieth birthday and my eighty-eighth birthday (Tokyo)

My parents' graves at Rookwood Cemetery in Sydney

STILL CAUSING TROUBLE

As I approach my ninetieth year, I still go into the office every day, the phone rings constantly with inquiries from old and new clients, I still see injustice around me, especially in the business world, and my passion for fighting it is undimmed.

In 2009 the National Australia Bank (NAB) announced a share purchase plan for existing shareholders which treated them as second-class corporate citizens, and I wrote to the *Australian Financial Review* in August of that year, to express my outrage. The paper titled my letter 'NAB Board's Utter Contempt':

> Loyal shareholders who had braved the depths of the global financial crisis in 2008 and suffered an initial loss of more than 10 per cent on their $10,000 contribution to NAB's coffers had their entitlement under the latest share purchase plan reduced to only one-third of that offered to shareholders who did not partake in the 2008 share offer.
>
> According to the information now provided by its share registry, no shareholder is to be allotted less than $500 worth of shares (about 22 shares) under the announced scale-back.
>
> How generous can you get? For a most reputable board to treat loyal shareholders with such utter contempt deserves the strongest

> condemnation and hopefully its actions will attract the attention of the corporate regulator.
>
> Shareholders who over decades have supported companies under often the most trying and adverse economic conditions deserve better. Share purchase plans that offer shareholders the crumbs left after institutions are given the cake have deteriorated into a farce.

My letter became known as the 'utter contempt' letter and received so much media coverage that the chairman of NAB, Michael Chaney, was made to apologise and accepted that in future, all shareholders must be treated equally. The AFR followed up with a strongly worded editorial, titled 'Small fry must not be ignored', which endorsed my arguments and criticised the bank and other institutions. I introduced myself to Michael Chaney at the NAB's subsequent annual general meeting and he was less than welcoming.

This said more about Chaney than about anything else. What matters, as it has always mattered to me over the years, is that I hope my contribution and ideas can lead to some benefit for the public. The response to my 'utter contempt' letter from another *Financial Review* reader sums this up nicely:

> Henri Aram's condemnation of the National Australia Bank Board for its 'utter contempt' in not providing all its shareholders with pro-rata entitlements should have appeared on the front page.
>
> I urge the media to take up Aram's call for regulation.

Barely two months later, one of the industry regulators, the Productivity Commission, released a proposal which had the potential to rip off investors even more insidiously.

It was called the 'two strikes' rule. If a company's remuneration report for its executive management receives a 'no' vote of 25 per cent or more at two consecutive annual general meetings, shareholders will have the opportunity to vote on a motion to spill the company's entire board.

I wrote to the Productivity Commission (and ASIC) in October 2009 to express my concern at this proposal:

> The process of voting against most remuneration reports to shareholders by the proxies of anonymous beneficial owners through Nominee companies, and in anticipation of your 'two-strike' rule, is already evident from recent results of highly regarded and well-managed industrials such as United Group (49% proxies), Downer EDI (69% largely proxies) and others.
>
> Once implemented, all these companies, the next time around in 2010–11, will be targeted by speculators, their share prices decimated and thousands of hapless investors – the mums and dads, the retirees (present and future) – will have their savings shredded, while the hedge funds and market spivs will laugh all the way to the bank!
>
> The costly, time-wasting and futile exercise, once completed, will have achieved nothing but the wealth destruction of all those whose fortunes had been tied to the ongoing success of the enterprise to which they had contributed and helped to build.

Although neither body replied to my argument, the proposal continued to receive coverage in the press. I maintained my rage with this letter to the *Australian Financial Review* in March 2010:

> The chairman of Foster's Group and Lend Lease, David Crawford, is one of many directors to complain about the growing influence of proxy advisers ... who advise major shareholders about how to vote at annual meetings.
>
> 'That in itself raises the question: are the institutional shareholders that are relying on these reports abdicating their responsibility?' Crawford reportedly said at an Australian Institute of Company Directors event in Melbourne to some applause.
>
> This novel and insidious practice not only raises the question posed by Crawford whether or not institutional shareholders are abdicating their responsibility, but the possibly more important one whether or not they breach Australian Stock Exchange rules whereby the market must be fully informed of market sensitive information.
>
> What could be more sensitive to stock prices than the possibility of a board having to resign as a result of a large percentage of proxies voting against a remuneration report in order to destabilise the board?
>
> This information often is in the hands of proxy advisers, often without notice to the board, let alone the investing public. Such information withheld from the market is the very fuel that ignites the short sellers and hedge funds to the detriment and losses of investors.

The business sector needs to set higher standards for its corporate behaviour and the government needs to think more laterally and with greater compassion. The current debate about asylum seekers bears uncanny similarities with the country that greeted my family when we arrived here 70 years ago, and brought to my mind a solution that borrows from my own wartime experience. The *Financial Review* thought the 'Aram Solution' was worth publishing, in May 2011:

> While increased migration and proposed participation reforms are long-term objectives, our needs are clearly urgent and near term. During the 1940s at the beginning of World War II, under a Labor Government refugees or 'reffos' who had fled the German Nazi regime became instant enemy aliens and as such were rounded up for internment. But instead of confined idleness in internment camps, they were drafted into labour corps and helped the war effort. Many of them became leaders in industry and were decorated for their services after the war.
>
> Seventy years on and in a more humane and enlightened society they are now classified as 'asylum seekers' who have fled war-torn countries for refuge on our shores, albeit illegally and by means of people smugglers. So be it.
>
> But they appear able-bodied and their individual skills have never been tested. With the imminent shortage of labour, why not likewise draft them into labour corps, declare an amnesty and, suitably supervised, afford them the opportunity of earning their future citizenship by contributing their brawn and most likely their brains to our economic benefits.
>
> Apart from any humanitarian considerations, this will assist our budget by saving taxpayers.

Politicians are always finding new ways to deal with old problems, and today they can call on amazing technology and communication tools to help them. But they still don't understand ethics and commonsense. That's something that can't be taught.

I find it hard to believe that in all the years since I arrived in this country, people are still as scared of foreigners as they were when I set foot here in the summer of 1939. They are still driven by prejudice and ignorance, and sadly, governments are just as prepared to cater to those forces as they did before and during World War II. Parliamentary debate in those years regarded those seeking refuge from a murderous Nazi regime as 'the scum of Europe' that should be debarred from entry – and many perished as a result.

Let us not forget also the Children's Transports where their parents, in the hope that their offspring might survive, put their children on trains to leave Germany during 1938–39. What is so different to the unaccompanied children, likewise relinquished by their parents for similar reasons and arriving here as boat people in 2011? The only difference, perhaps, is that they are to be deported to another country in spite of the hazards and risks to their existence. While we deplore people smugglers, the present government has become itself a people shuffler, although the High Court rejecting the so-called Malaysian Solution has found against such repugnant practice and forced the government to think again.

In this country we have seen, over three generations, what a positive and rewarding difference refugees have made to our society. The reasons people flee their homes are, to this day, the same as always: escaping wars, conflicts and abuse of human rights. From the Eastern and Southern Europeans in the late 1930s to the 1950s, through to Vietnamese in the 1970s and Chinese after Tiananmen Square. They all worked hard, and within a generation they and their families have integrated and enriched Australia in their chosen professions and in commerce.

From early in my youth, our parents instilled in us their own conviction that became a sort of family motto: 'Live and Let Live.' I have tried to abide by this dictum and hope to have achieved their example. Australia has been my lucky country. I celebrate the good fortune I have enjoyed, the pleasure I derive from helping others, and the freedom I have to speak up on behalf of those who can't.

THE ARAM FAMILY TREE

Julius Abraham (1876) married Rosa Riesenfeld (1895)
Changed name to Aram (1931)

ARNOLD (1921)

Married Yuki (1962)

Anthony (m. Masako)

Ayuko (b. 2000)

Alexander (m. So Myung)

Hana (b. 2000)
Ina (b. 2003)

HEINZ (HENRI) (1923)

Married 1. Ilse (Strasser) 1949-53

Married 2. Christina (Nieke) 1962-83

Jackie (b. 1972; m. Ian 2005)
Evelyn Christine (b. 2009)

Married 3. Robin (Stokes) 1999-
(two sons from previous marriage)

Marcus (m. Jen)
Benjamin (b. 1999)
Imogen (b. 2006)
Lillian (b. 2009)

Jason (m. Vicki)
Anika (b. 2004)
Hayden (b. 2006)
Korbin (b.2008)
Rhylan (b. 2010)

INDEX

References to photos are in italic font. HA's activities have been grouped under headings such as 'education', 'letter-writing and campaigns' and 'work'. HA = Henri Aram.